AIMR Conference Proceedings

Fixed-Income Management: Credit, Covenants, and Core-Plus

Proceedings of the AIMR seminar "Fixed-Income Management 2002—Innovation Continues." AIMR hosts a conference annually on fixed income. Visit www.aimr.org/conferences/ for more information on this yearly conference, normally held in the early fall.

25–26 September 2002
Boston

Charles B. Burkhart, Jr.
Peter J. Chirlian
R.B. Davidson III
Robin L. Diamonte
Mohamed A. El-Erian
Christopher L. Gootkind, CFA
Scott E. Grannis
James Grant
Stephen Kealhofer
Abigail L. McKenna, CFA
Kenneth R. Meyer
William L. Nemerever, CFA, *moderator*
Kevin J. Perry
Marc P. Seidner, CFA
Robert F. Shainheit
Kathleen M. Shanley, CFA
Kurt D. Winkelmann

Association for Investment Management and Research®

Dedicated to the Highest Standards of Ethics, Education, and Professional Practice in Investment Management and Research.

To obtain an *AIMR Product Catalog*, contact
AIMR, 560 Ray C. Hunt Drive, Charlottesville, Virginia 22903, U.S.A.
Phone 434-951-5499; Fax 434-951-5262; E-mail info@aimr.org
or
visit AIMR's Web site at www.aimr.org
to view the AIMR publications list.

AIMR CONFERENCE PROCEEDINGS
(USPS 013-739 ISSN 1535-0207) 2003

Is published five times a year in March, April, twice in August, and September, by the Association for Investment Management and Research at 560 Ray C. Hunt Drive, Charlottesville, VA. **Periodical postage paid at Charlottesville, Virginia, and additional mailing offices.**

Copies are mailed as a benefit of membership to CFA® charterholders. Subscriptions also are available at $100.00 USA. For one year. Address all circulation communications to AIMR Conference Proceedings, 560 Ray C. Hunt Drive, Charlottesville, Virginia 22903, USA; Phone 434-951-5499; Fax 434-951-5262. For change of address. Send mailing label and new address six weeks in advance.

Postmaster: Please send address changes to AIMR Conference Proceedings, Association for Investment Management and Research, P.O. Box 3668, Charlottesville, Virginia 22903.

ISBN 0-935015-88-4
Printed in the United States of America
February 10, 2003

Contents

Selected Publications

AIMR

Benchmarks and Attribution Analysis, 2001

Best Execution and Portfolio Performance, 2001

Core-Plus Bond Management, 2001

Developments in Quantitative Investment Models, 2001

Equity Portfolio Construction, 2002

Equity Research and Valuation Techniques, 2002

Evolution in Equity Markets: Focus on Asia, 2001

Fixed-Income Management for the 21st Century, 2002

Hedge Fund Management, 2002

Investment Counseling for Private Clients III, 2001

Investment Counseling for Private Clients IV, 2002

Investment Firms: Trends and Issues, 2001

Organizational Challenges for Investment Firms, 2002

Research Foundation

Anomalies and Efficient Portfolio Formation, 2002
by S.P. Kothari and Jay Shanken

The Closed-End Fund Discount, 2002
by Elroy Dimson and Carolina Minio-Paluello

Common Determinants of Liquidity and Trading, 2001
by Tarun Chordia, Richard Roll, and Avanidhar Subrahmanyam

Country, Sector, and Company Factors in Global Equity Portfolios, 2001
by Peter J.B. Hopkins and C. Hayes Miller, CFA

International Financial Contagion: Theory and Evidence in Evolution, 2002
by Roberto Rigobon

Real Options and Investment Valuation, 2002
by Don M. Chance, CFA, and Pamela P. Peterson, CFA

Risk Management, Derivatives, and Financial Analysis under SFAS No. 133, 2001
by Gary L. Gastineau, Donald J. Smith, and Rebecca Todd, CFA

The Role of Monetary Policy in Investment Management, 2000
by Gerald R. Jensen, Robert R. Johnson, CFA, and Jeffrey M. Mercer

Term-Structure Models Using Binomial Trees, 2001
by Gerald W. Buetow, Jr., CFA, and James Sochacki

Authors

We would like to thank William L. Nemerever, CFA, of Grantham, Mayo, Van Otterloo & Company, LLC, for serving as moderator at this conference. Also, we extend our appreciation to James H. Gilkeson, CFA, of the University of Central Florida, for serving as guest content editor and writing the overview for this proceedings. Finally, we wish to express our sincere gratitude to the authors listed below for their contributions to both the conference and this proceedings:

R.B. Davidson III is director of the Municipal Bond Department at Bernstein Investment Research and Management, where he serves as chairman of the Tax-Exempt Fixed-Income Policy Group. Previously, he served as vice president and head of municipal strategies at J.P. Morgan Securities and was an associate economist at Lehman Brothers. Mr. Davidson has authored several journal articles and was named to the Institutional Investor All-America Research Team. He holds a B.A. from Wesleyan University and an M.B.A. from the Stern School of Business at New York University.

Mohamed A. El-Erian is managing director and a senior member of Pacific Investment Management Company's portfolio management and investment strategy group, where he is also head of the firm's emerging market portfolio management team. Previously, he headed the emerging markets economic research team at Salomon Smith Barney/Citibank. Mr. El-Erian has written on the topic of international economics and has appeared on CNN, CNBC, and Reuters and Bloomberg television. He holds an undergraduate degree from Cambridge University and doctoral and master's degrees from Oxford University.

Christopher L. Gootkind, CFA, is vice president and director of fixed-income research at Wellington Management Company, LLP, where he manages the credit research process and oversees analysts involved in the credit analysis of domestic and international bond issuers in all market sectors. Previously, he served as director of fixed-income credit research at Scudder Kemper Investments, where he developed the firm's asset-backed securities research effort and managed a large institutional corporate bond portfolio. Mr. Gootkind holds a B.A. in mathematics from Williams College and an M.B.A. with a concentration in finance and investment management from Harvard University.

Scott E. Grannis is director and chief economist at Western Asset Management Company, where he is responsible for developing the firm's domestic and international outlook and specializes in Federal Reserve policy analysis and interest rate forecasting. Previously, he served as senior economist at the Claremont Economics Institute, an economic forecasting and consulting service. Mr. Grannis is the author of numerous papers on monetary, economic, and financial market issues and has been quoted in such publications as the *Wall Street Journal*, *Fortune*, and *Business Week*. He holds a B.A. in philosophy from Pomona College and an M.B.A. from Claremont Graduate University.

Stephen Kealhofer is managing director at Moody's KMV, where he serves on the board of directors and is cohead of research. Previously, he served as director of research for Diversified Corporate Loans. Mr. Kealhofer has taught investment management and corporate finance at Columbia University and the University of California at Berkeley. He holds a B.A. in economics from Macalester College and a Ph.D. in economics from Princeton University.

Abigail L. McKenna, CFA, is managing director at Morgan Stanley Investment Management and is a portfolio manager for their emerging markets debt portfolio. Previously, she served as a senior portfolio manager at MIMCO and was a limited partner and portfolio manager at Weiss Peck & Greer. Ms. McKenna is a chairperson of the Emerging Markets Creditor's Association and a director of the Emerging Markets Traders Association. She holds a B.A. in international relations from Georgetown University.

Kenneth R. Meyer is chairman, CEO, and managing director of Lincoln Capital Management Company. Previously, he served as senior vice president at the Harris Bank, where he was responsible for institutional asset management. Mr. Meyer is a director of Irish Life of North America and LINK Unlimited, a minority education program. He is a graduate of the University of Notre Dame and holds an M.B.A. from the Wharton School of the University of Pennsylvania.

Kevin J. Perry is vice president and portfolio manager of Loomis, Sayles & Company, LP, where he is responsible for the management of bank loan assets. Previously, he held senior positions at The Pilgrim Group and Baring Asset Management. Mr. Perry holds a B.S. in business administration from Lowell

Technological Institute and an M.B.A. from Boston University.

Kathleen M. Shanley, CFA, is senior corporate bond analyst at Gimme Credit, Inc., a leading independent provider of high-grade and crossover taxable corporate bond research for institutional investors. Her responsibilities include coverage of such high-grade financials as banks, securities firms, and insurance companies. Previously, Ms. Shanley served as vice president in the corporate bond research group of BankAmerica Corporation. She holds a B.S. from Georgetown University and an M.B.A from the Wharton School of the University of Pennsylvania.

Overview

James H. Gilkeson, CFA
Associate Professor of Finance
University of Central Florida
Orlando, Florida

"May you live in interesting times" is a well-known expression popularly attributed to a so-called ancient Chinese curse. The phrase wisely suggests that events that are entertaining to outsiders or exciting to us in hindsight can be quite painful while we live through them. (The only problem is that the curse is neither Chinese nor very old. It dates back to a short story published in the April 1950 issue of *Astounding Science Fiction*. Apparently, the author thought the phrase would have more weight if it bore an exotic philosophical label.)[1]

It is easy these days for fixed-income managers to feel cursed. They do indeed live in "interesting times," with interest rates at record lows, defaults at record highs, and the U.S. and global economies facing continuing uncertainty. The initial impulse might be to dwell on the irresistible nature of the situation, give it an ancient philosophical label, and wait for it to end. But volatile times offer opportunities. As Kenneth Meyer noted in the conference's opening keynote address, "Fixed-income managers . . . should remember that change is how they make their money and how they add value to client portfolios." The key is to identify important changes in the marketplace, recognize the value that can be created, and act accordingly.

Bravery in the New World

What characterizes the current fixed-income marketplace? According to Kenneth Meyer, there is a lot of bad news out there—but a number of opportunities exist as well. The bad news has become familiar: low interest rates, minuscule inflation, and rising corporate and consumer default rates. Perhaps the only good news has been that equity markets have tanked as well. Meyer believes that many of tomorrow's fixed-income managers will find themselves following enhanced-index or core-plus mandates with low fees but moderate return goals. In this part of the business, size will dominate because of the need for computational power and data resources. But he suggests that many opportunities exist for specialists to fill niches in the market. Skills and abilities worth developing are found in the areas of customized portfolio structures, quantitative research, risk management and risk budgeting, applying recent advances in finance theory, and new fixed-income instruments.

Credit Analysis

Given the rise in corporate defaults over the past two years, it is critical to re-emphasize good credit analysis. Kathleen Shanley reminds us that a key ingredient to building a successful portfolio and generating alpha is to select strong issuers. Although new techniques for credit analysis have been introduced in recent years, in many cases, the best approach is to go back to the basics and focus on earnings, liquidity, leverage, and so on. Management pronouncements need to be viewed through a skeptical lens. Investors need to *read* the source documents carefully, rather than relying on managers to highlight important information. Yesterday's disclosure problems should not be forgotten tomorrow.

Shanley notes that credit analysts need to be aware of rating triggers and the role of rating agencies. Rating agencies have found themselves in a "damned if you do, damned if you don't" situation because of the proliferation of rating triggers, particularly in bank loans. A rating trigger is a specific action (e.g., an increase in a loan rate or cancellation of a line of credit) that will occur if an issuer's debt rating drops below a certain level, usually below investment grade. A downgrade from Baa to Ba may trigger further problems that may lead to a further decline in the credit rating. On the one hand, if a rating agency reduces an issuer's rating, it can be accused of helping to cause a default because the action sets off the rating trigger. On the other hand, if the agency delays reducing a company's rating because of a rating trigger, it can be accused of failing in its monitoring duty.

Shanley also points out that fixed-income analysts need to pay a bit less attention to equity market prices. This advice is based on a number of factors, including the well-known fact that equity holders have an option on upside gains, whereas creditors do

[1] For an interesting story of one man's attempt to determine the origin of this "ancient Chinese curse," read Stephen DeLong's account at http://hawk.fab2.albany.edu/sidebar/sidebar.htm.

not, and the fact that managers may sometimes take actions that benefit shareholders at the expense of bondholders. Although credit analysis and equity analysis share some common ground, one cannot substitute for the other.

Stephen Kealhofer's presentation provides an overview of KMV's approach to portfolio credit risk measurement. The approach is based on the distance to default—that is, the distance between an issuer's current market value of assets and the issuer's default point (typically when assets fall to about 75 percent of liabilities). The likelihood of default is based on this distance and on the volatility of asset values, adjusted for the fact that changes in asset values are not normally distributed. The KMV approach uses market data about a company's equity value and volatility to impute the market value of assets and its volatility.

A key step in the KMV process is to determine the correlations between the asset values of individual issuers, which is equivalent to estimating the joint probability distribution of the asset values. Once this determination is made, the model can measure default expectations for the portfolio and optimize the risk–return trade-off. Using this framework, Kealhofer provides evidence of the substantial diversification benefits that are available and the risk reduction that can be obtained. In the KMV model, the most important characteristic of an individual security is its "risk contribution" to the portfolio. The fundamental insights gained from the model are that fixed-income managers need to hold more assets than are typical to obtain full diversification benefits and that common fixed-income benchmarks provide far less than optimal diversification.

Creditor Rights

Both Abigail McKenna and Christopher Gootkind discuss the state of creditor rights. McKenna focuses on creditor rights problems for emerging market debt. In recent years, when demand for securities often outstripped supply, fixed-income managers tended to buy what they could get. These managers need to read bond contracts and understand their terms and conditions. Also, recent history suggests that creditors must learn to live with high credit rating volatility.

According to McKenna, creditors are particularly vulnerable to restructurings. Borrowers in crisis avoid talking with creditors and frequently pit them against each other. Foreign bondholders are de facto subordinated investors—behind local investors and the international financial institutions, such as the International Monetary Fund (IMF) and the World Bank. Emerging market debt tends to contain few covenants, and foreign investors have little power to protect their interests. There is no sovereign debt equivalent to U.S. bankruptcy proceedings, and investors cannot assume that all claims will be treated fairly.

McKenna discusses proposals for dealing with emerging market debt restructurings that are offered by three bodies—the Emerging Market Creditors Association (EMCA), the G–10, and the IMF. Of the three groups, EMCA seems the most viable because it is composed of major institutional investors who collectively have the clout to affect emerging market debt structures. EMCA also allows investors to speak to issuers for themselves rather than relying on investment banks to represent their interests, and it enables them to share information with each another.

Gootkind concentrates on creditor rights issues in investment-grade bond markets. Recent high-profile defaults by major U.S. bond issuers and numerous downgrades have raised concerns about fraud, lack of clear disclosure, and priority of claims in bankruptcy. They have also caused investors to focus on their rights, as spelled out in the indenture and as experienced in actual defaults.

Creditor rights are spelled out in the indenture in the form of covenants meant to protect bondholders. Recent actions by issuers such as AK Steel, Rite Aid, and Owens Illinois, however, show that covenants may offer less protection than might be imagined after a cursory reading and can be changed using somewhat coercive methods.

Gootkind offers a list of covenants that investors ought to insist on, including strong negative pledges, springing liens, debt and minimum-net-worth tests, asset sale limitations, rating-trigger limitations, and limits on off-balance-sheet debt. He also discusses the roles of informal and formal creditor committees. Informal committees can have a positive impact (e.g., Owens Illinois) but have no legal standing. Formal committees exercise more power in a bankruptcy, but membership on such a committee may prove difficult if an investment manager has clients with competing interests in the issuer.

Changing Core-Plus Mandates

In years past, when fixed-income returns were high and equity returns were even higher, fixed-income managers and their clients tended to focus on returns and forget about safety. Given recent history, many clients will return to the old focus, with a stronger interest in secure returns from their fixed-income portfolios. Core-plus mandates will likely remain, but excess return expectations will be more reasonable.

Scott Grannis' presentation highlights fundamental changes in the fixed-income world. The Lehman Brothers U.S. Aggregate Index has experienced a massive evolution during the last 15 or so years, moving from being dominated by U.S. Treasury securities in 1985 (49 percent of the index) to holding more complex instruments. In 2002, corporate bonds and mortgage securities made up 60 percent of the index and Treasuries only 22 percent. In addition, the corporate sector contains a much higher concentration of lower-grade (BBB rated) securities than it once did.

As Grannis points out, a fixed-income portfolio is developed from two distinct investment decisions, one on duration and one on credit risk. Both are becoming more difficult, as long-term securities disappear from the benchmarks and credit ratings become more volatile. The growing importance of mortgage-related securities and Treasury Inflation-Indexed Securities (also known as TIPS) brings new challenges, particularly with interest rates and inflation at record lows.

The key to earning core-plus returns will be tactical allocations to nonbenchmark sectors, such as nondollar bonds, emerging market debt, and high-yield debt. Managers also need the ability to use derivatives, especially for duration management.

Opportunities in Nonbenchmark Sectors

Mohamed El-Erian and Kevin Perry's presentations discuss opportunities in nonbenchmark sectors. El-Erian makes the case for adding emerging market debt to fixed-income portfolios. Emerging market debt has offered exceptional returns and low correlations with other sectors, leading to good diversification benefits in recent years. Further, despite high volatility as a result of a spate of high-profile problems in Mexico, Russia, Argentina, and other countries, volatility-adjusted returns for the asset class have been strong.

Emerging market debt investments require a fundamentals-based approach. Each credit should be acceptable on a stand-alone basis. Key attributes to consider are the country's internal fundamentals, its external environment, and the technical strength of its debt relative to both competing and complementary asset classes. El-Erian also provides an overview of the current market outlook, highlighting the importance of global risk aversion and the health of the U.S. economy. The emerging market debt sector is anchored by good policies, a growing investor base, and improving information quality. Although the current outlook is a bit rocky, it deserves a place in core-plus portfolios.

Perry focuses our attention on the high-yield sector, which has become a permanent feature of the fixed-income landscape. The sector has been battered in recent years, with high defaults and poor returns, but continues to offer good long-term return and diversification benefits. Structural changes, including quicker reactions by rating agencies and a reduction in liquidity, have led to higher volatility in the sector.

A bright spot in the high-yield debt sector is leveraged bank loans. Bank loans have many advantages over high-yield bonds, including tighter covenants, shorter effective lives, and (typically) the most senior spot on the issuer's capital structure. The market for these instruments is growing, liquidity has increased, pricing transparency has improved, and transactions are becoming standardized. Risk-adjusted returns have been extraordinary over the past 10 years, with no negative return years. The sector has also maintained low correlations with other asset classes. In short, leveraged bank loans provide an ideal core-plus investment that offers reduced portfolio volatility and enhanced returns.

And Remember Municipals

R.B. Davidson advocates the inclusion of taxable bonds in taxable portfolios to execute optimal duration strategies and achieve the highest after-tax return available in a given market environment. Municipal bond portfolio managers can get ahead of the competition by taking advantage of two very basic concepts: exploiting the tax code (tactical repositioning between the taxable and tax-exempt bond markets) and broadening the investment universe beyond the client's home state to a national municipal bond portfolio. Two exceptions, the states of New York and California, exist for the latter tenet. Active tax management, such as harvesting losses and holding gains until long term, can also add significant after-tax excess return. Still a challenge, however, is the lack of a good after-tax performance benchmark and after-tax performance measurement tools.

Conclusion

So, we find ourselves in the midst of interesting times in the fixed-income markets—low interest rates, high default rates, periods of high volatility, and increasingly concentrated benchmarks. Our conference speakers offer a range of remedies to squeeze out every ounce of excess return that the fixed-income market has to offer. Strengthening the core portfolio through an emphasis on fundamental credit analysis sets the groundwork. Joining with other bond buyers to demand tight bond covenants and enforce creditor rights adds another layer of protection. Expanding the investment universe to include noncore sectors, such as leveraged bank loans, emerging market debt, and high yield, can enhance fixed-income performance even further. The theme of a broader universe holds true for tax-exempt bond portfolios as well—encompassing both a national municipal portfolio and the taxable bond market.

A CEO's Perspective on the Challenges in Fixed-Income Management

Kenneth R. Meyer
Chairman, CEO, and Managing Director
Lincoln Capital Management Company
Chicago

The main challenge for fixed-income managers is to differentiate themselves from their competitors while adding value for clients. This task has been complicated by recent changes in the fixed-income market (particularly lower interest rates). In the future, success in fixed-income management will depend on a firm's ability to adapt to and exploit changes in several key areas: enhanced-index/core-plus structures, specialty manager roles, customized portfolio management, quantitative research, risk management and risk budgets, advances in financial theory, and sophisticated financial instruments.

Active fixed-income managers face considerable challenges. Market rates are at historic lows, credit spreads are widening and erratic, management fees are declining, and competition is rising. This presentation examines the current state of the fixed-income management business, its future direction, and how firms can differentiate themselves in an increasingly difficult environment.

A Changed Environment

The world has changed over the past year. Fixed-income managers, rather than wringing their hands over recent experiences, should remember that change is how they make their money and how they add value to client portfolios—by taking advantage of change, thinking about it, doing research, and creating opportunity. How managers respond to change differentiates them from each other and determines whether value is added to or subtracted from clients' portfolios. The magnitude of value that can be gained or lost from these types of opportunities has increased substantially.

The 10-year yield for U.S. T-bonds fell below 4 percent in March 2002. Inflation is roughly 1 percent, an unprecedented level, at least within recent history. The combination of low interest rates (read low actuarial assumptions or low income returns) and recent poor returns on other assets will quickly put serious cost pressures on both large defined-benefit plans as well as foundation portfolios. So, clients are looking to investment management firms for creative solutions.

Low interest rates have also created some unusual incentives for consumers as well as for the lenders who cater to them. Both consumers and credit card issuers have taken advantage of low interest rates and easy credit. As indicated in **Figure 1**, credit card solicitations in 2001 were close to $5 billion. The bad news is that default rates also rose sharply, to almost 7 percent. When Capital One Bank reported its earnings in early September 2002, it estimated that 40 percent of its credit card balances were subprime. Needless to say, we can expect default rates to jump higher if even a whiff of a recession occurs in the near future.

The expansion of consumer debt has gone far beyond the credit card. The mortgage market is now larger than the U.S. Treasury market, as indicated in **Figure 2**. But not to worry—the combination of funding the Homeland Security Agency, a possible war, and the prospect of pulling the economy out of a recession will put the Treasury back in the issuing lead in the not-too-distant future.

Corporate management, particularly those associated with the likes of WorldCom, Tyco International, and Conseco, have been equally adept at responding to low interest rates and easy credit

Figure 1. Solicitations and Default Rate for U.S. Credit Card Market, 1991–2001

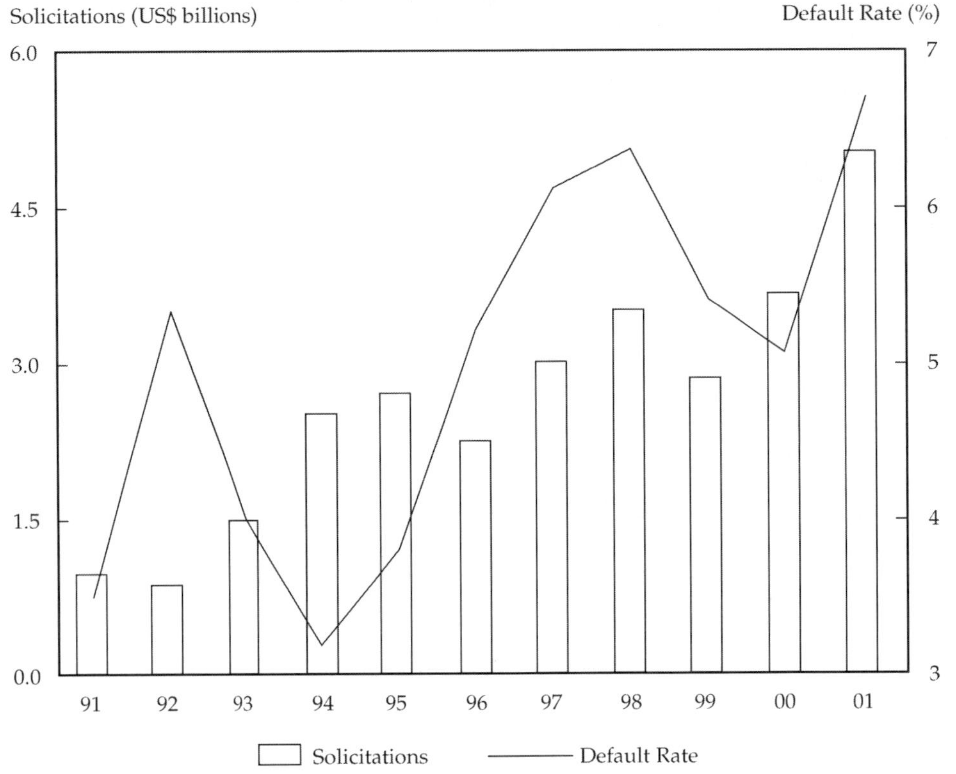

Source: Based on data from Carrick Molenkamp, "Credit-Card Scrutiny Hits Lenders and Threatens to Damp Spending," *Wall Street Journal* (19 August 2002).

Figure 2. Mortgage-Related Debt versus Treasuries, 1990–2002

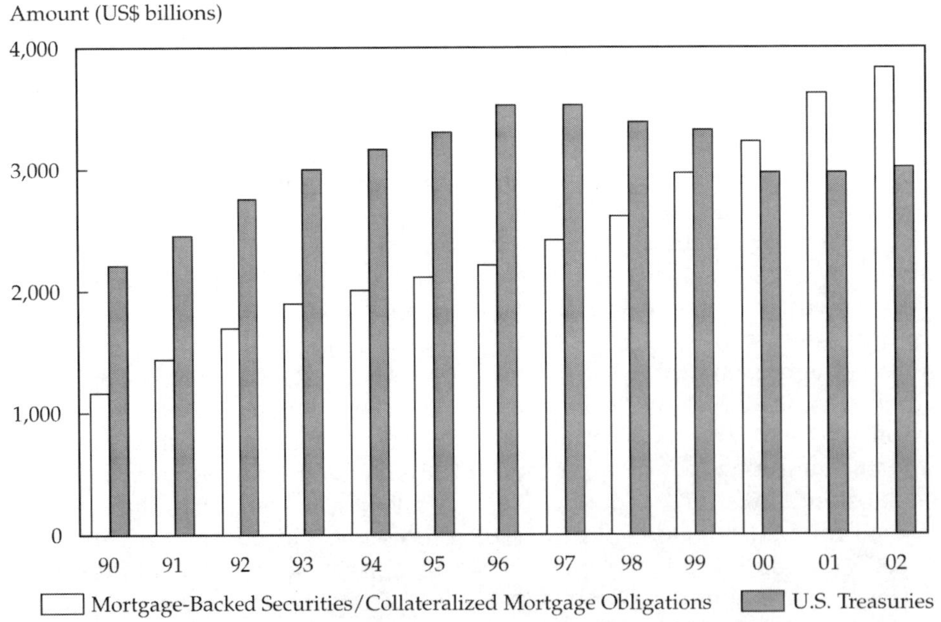

Source: Based on data from Gregory Zukerman, "Refinancing Rocks Bond Market," *Wall Street Journal* (8 August 2002).

conditions by issuing more debt. Management compensation has been geared almost entirely to short-term movements in stock prices; thus, many corporate managers simply did what they were being paid to do. The fallout, however, was such that bondholders and shareholders will not forget the devastation for a long time. The recent abuses have had, and will continue to have, a serious impact on how fixed-income portfolios are managed.

Consider the short-term impact. Lehman Brothers estimated a credit sector excess return of –259 bps for the month of July 2002. That is the bad news. The good news is that other equally painful return months have occurred in the past:

February 1933	–265 bps
March 1971	–268 bps
October 1987	–291 bps
September 1971	–306 bps
March 1966	–355 bps
April 1932	–780 bps

Not only did corporate spreads widen, but volatility within the sector also increased.

Table 1 compares the distribution of option-adjusted spreads for A rated corporate bonds in December 1997 with those of August 2002. In August, 80 percent of A rated corporates had spreads of 200 bps or greater, and 24 percent had spreads of 300 bps or greater. Five years ago, in December 1997, 95 percent of A rated corporates had spreads of 100 bps or less. Not only have A rated spreads widened, but the spreads between good and bad credits have widened sharply as well.

Table 1. Option-Adjusted Spread Distribution for A Rated Corporates over Treasuries, August 2002 versus December 1997

Spread	December 1997	August 2002
100 bps	95%	20%
200	4	56
300	1	13
300+	0	11

Source: Based on data from Lincoln Capital Management Company and Lehman Brothers.

The credit sector impact on active portfolio returns has been dramatic. Using Callan Associates published manager return data, we estimated that for the year ending 30 June 2002, 67 percent of active fixed-income managers underperformed the Lehman Aggregate, adjusted for fees. We assumed a fee differential of 20 bps between active and passive management and adjusted the data accordingly. Whether the measurement period is one year, three years, five years, or seven years, the conclusion remains the same: A passive index return has exceeded most active manager returns.

The point is not that active management is good or bad but that underperformance is a hurdle that must be overcome as active managers look toward the future. Our clients are well aware of this problem and are looking for alternatives. The challenge is to reassess the future of our business. It is a business that, judging from the current low level of rates, has a very good chance of delivering high absolute returns. But it is also a business that has not consistently delivered acceptable relative returns.

Right or wrong, the fixed-income asset class is going to receive a lot of attention as an alternative to common stocks over the next couple of years. This is particularly true for the defined-contribution sector, in which investments are directed by individual owners. We need to be ready for that attention.

2002 and Beyond

Several factors or trends will affect, if not define, the immediate future of the fixed-income management business:

- the increasing use of enhanced-index/core-plus structures;
- specialty manager roles, particularly for higher-risk, higher-return fixed-asset categories;
- customized portfolio structures;
- increased use of quantitative research;
- better risk management tools;
- the imposition of risk budgets by clients;
- advances in financial theory; and
- the continued growth of more sophisticated financial instruments.

Enhanced-Index/Core-Plus Structures. Active managers have not delivered returns that consistently exceed the returns of alternative passive strategies net of fees. According to Callan Associates data for manager returns through 30 June 2002 (adjusted for fees), roughly two-thirds to three-quarters of these managers delivered below-market returns. Not surprisingly, institutional clients have already moved a large amount of money to passive and enhanced-index/core-plus structures. Poor relative returns to date in 2002 assure that this trend will continue, if not accelerate.

Enhanced-index/core-plus structures can be broadly defined by three factors: moderate return goals, low fees, and well-defined (often quantitatively driven) portfolio strategies.

■ *Moderate return goals.* These structures normally offer relatively moderate return goals—goals that also happen to have the added advantage of being achievable. A typical goal would be 15–25 bps in excess of a broad market benchmark net of fees. These types of returns would have ranked in the upper quartile of actively managed portfolios over the past five to seven years.

Properly managed enhanced-index portfolios should also incorporate some sort of downside risk protection. This risk protection can significantly reduce the probability of a portfolio return below the index. Fixed-income assets are normally held to moderate overall portfolio risk, one element of which is less volatile, more predictable returns. When we fail to deliver that predictability, clients are sorely disappointed.

■ *Low fees.* With the large accounts that typically invest in these types of structures, the client is able to beat down fixed-income managers' fees. Obviously, low fees are attractive to clients, and competition will keep driving them lower.

■ *Portfolio strategy.* Enhanced indexing is not a simple buy-and-hold strategy—a fact that is all the more evident now that the likes of Worldcom, Tyco, and Dynegy have wreaked their havoc on all of us. Those troubled bonds often carry very high current yields. That high current income has, as they say, "street appeal." Unfortunately, that same high current income must be matched or exceeded in the passive or enhanced portfolio as long as those issuers' bonds remain in the index to produce a competitive income.

The challenge to portfolio managers is, of course, that a credit downgrade to junk status can wipe out a year or more of added value. A 500 bp spread widening on a 1–2 percent position will cost 5–10 bps of total return. Today's credit environment is harsh. Poor credit decisions are severely penalized. But this is not the first time, nor will it be the last time, that these conditions have existed. Intense credit research, diversification, and even a touch of active portfolio management are all necessary components of a well-designed enhanced-index strategy.

The enhanced-index business is tough and is becoming more complex. Lincoln Capital Management Company has invested a tremendous amount of money in technology to cope with and improve our ability to use increasingly complex and sophisticated instruments.

Total-return swaps are just one example. On occasion, these swaps have enabled investors to lock in a positive yield spread on a portfolio position; this is a perfect example of how to add value in an enhanced-index portfolio. Cash and commercial mortgage-backed securities (CMBS) positions are sold and a one-month LIBOR floater at 10 bps over LIBOR is purchased. Simultaneously, a total-return swap is entered into. The swap consists of buying the return of the CMBS benchmark for a period of time from a dealer. The cost is the one-month LIBOR rate less 45 bps. The net return to the portfolio for this position is 55 bps. Such a transaction, however, entails many potential risks that have to be managed, including counterparty risk and liquidity.

The point is that the enhanced-index business is more complex today than it was six months ago and will continue to become more complex. It is not a buy-and-hold business.

Specialty Manager Roles. As the fixed-income management business evolves, some firms will provide core-type products and others will provide the risk-oriented components of a portfolio for which clients will pay higher fees in expectation of higher returns. Core-active management with full fees is a difficult business to break into. As discussed earlier, historically poor relative returns alone make it a tough sale. In addition, it is a business that is now dominated by a few very big players. Specialty fixed-income management, on the other hand, is a fertile area for a new fixed-income firm or for the redirection of an existing firm. It provides a firm with an array of opportunities to distinguish itself from others.

Specialized asset management is particularly suited for such categories as distressed debt, bank loans, high yield, emerging markets, or long-duration credit portfolios.

Customized Portfolio Management. Often, clients will isolate a segment of their portfolios to meet a particular need. In the early 1980s, credit-stressed companies (yes, they did exist then too) discovered the pension fund as a significant source of improved cash flow. They were able to lock in portfolio yields significantly higher than their actuarial assumptions. Those actuarial assumptions were then raised, which resulted in lower pension expenses and improved cash flow. The dedicated, cash flow matched, and immunized portfolio structures required to lock in these returns were the first truly customized portfolio structures. Actually, the first such structures were designed in the mid-1970s for two healthy companies in Chicago—RR Donnelley & Sons Company and Trans Union Corporation. Neither was a troubled company. Both companies, however, genuinely appreciated the present value of current expense reduction associated with more predictable returns versus possible lower future contributions resulting from higher, but more volatile, equity returns.

The introduction and increasing depth of the derivatives market—in particular, the futures and swap markets—have enabled portfolio managers to become even more creative in designing customized solutions. Some clients have sought to lock in the higher yields created by the combination of a sharply sloped yield curve and wide credit spreads. The simple approach would be to acquire a portfolio of non-Treasury securities that maximizes current yield. One strategy would be to use all non-U.S. Treasury securities for the obvious reason of buying higher yields. The non-U.S. Treasury securities, however, would need to have a relatively short duration because the last thing a manager wants is to combine the risks of a change in credit spreads with a change in rates in one security. So, the solution is to buy a short-duration bond; lever it with a series of futures, forwards, and swaps to build a 20-year duration exposure; charge relatively low fees; and then manage the portfolio over time to add a bit more value.

Quantitative Research. The common denominator in much of the preceding discussion is the role of quantitative research. In my personal opinion, quantitative research will be the factor that differentiates good fixed-income managers from average managers. It provides a mental discipline crucial to modeling current and past behavior, modeling cash flows, extrapolating patterns into the future, and making portfolio decisions. Quantitative analytics is by no means the answer to all of our prayers, but it sure beats seat-of-the-pants decision making.

Risk Management and Risk Budgets. Risk budgeting is a perfect example of the useful application of quantitative analytics to the portfolio management process. The true definition of risk for most clients (and thus for most managers as well) is to experience a return below the benchmark or an absolute negative return. No one has ever complained about high risk-adjusted returns. (Actually, they have, but not for long.) How many times in your own organization have you looked at the quarterly rate of return for a portfolio, observed that it exceeded the performance of all other prior periods, and worried much about it? But if that same period return was negative, how much time would you spend beating on the desk and complaining that the pricing service "is no good this month"?

Managers now have tools that can help them assess how willing clients are to take on risk. Clients' circumstances and needs change, however, so the risk-assessment process needs to be fluid. Risk management will be an extraordinarily important part of our business going forward. The good news is that the academic and investment communities have made great strides in developing new analytical tools. So much more data are available today than just 5 or 10 years ago. And, of course, computational power has exploded.

Advances in Financial Theory. We managers do need to keep current on research advances in academia and how they might be applied in our business. For example, new academic research has enabled us to conduct conditional forecasting that we think (and that the academics think) provides better models to work with in the future, not only for interest rates but for yield spreads as well. These models use historical data but are capable of conditioning forecasted outcomes on a specified current market environment. One promising subject of academic research, extreme value theory, tells us how to adjust our models for these not-as-unlikely-as-we-thought events. Understanding and applying this new research will differentiate a manager from other fixed-income managers in terms of greater sophistication and the ability to add more value.

Sophisticated Financial Instruments. The number of instruments available for managers to enhance value—and, more important, to protect value—continues to increase. Managers should take time to learn how to use futures and other derivatives in their portfolios. Moreover, managers should not let clients prevent them from using futures or other derivatives. Many clients do not understand these instruments because they have little experience with them. Gaining permission to use such instruments and using them correctly will help managers differentiate themselves from their competitors.

Conclusion

Fixed-income managers need to focus on the future direction of the business. The key task for managers and firms is to differentiate themselves from their competitors while adding value for their clients. Enhanced-index products, customized structures, and faster computers can be used to control risk and add return. Managers can give themselves a competitive edge by appropriately using derivatives and other sophisticated financial instruments and by taking advantage of new academic and quantitative research. The fixed-income market is changing, but managers should think of change as fun. Remember, change is how we make money.

Question and Answer Session

Kenneth R. Meyer

Question: Is the Lehman Aggregate a fair benchmark?

Meyer: It is difficult to replicate a broad market index containing 5,000–6,000 bonds. An index is simply a set of bonds, which, in turn, is a set of cash flows. To replicate the benchmark, you need only replicate those cash flows, which is easier said than done. Those cash flows need to be option-adjusted, call-adjusted, and on and on. In a simpler fixed-income world, you might be able to replicate a benchmark with as few as 65 corporate issues and 10–12 Treasury issues. Today, it takes as many as 160–170 corporate issues.

Question: Given the specific risk in corporates, should managers avoid them?

Meyer: No, because the yield spread is simply too great. The competitive disadvantage of owning a lower-yielding portfolio is difficult to recoup.

Question: What should be the role of private-placement debt in the fixed-income structure mix, and do your clients allow private placements?

Meyer: Our clients do not allow private placements, except for Rule 144(a) securities. For large funds with well-diversified portfolios, private placements can be an important fixed-income asset category. Just do your homework in hiring a qualified private-placement manager.

Question: What types of quantitative management do you consider most valuable to managers?

Meyer: Some of the work being done in the credit area is valuable. Credit Suisse First Boston and others have done a lot of work relating stock price movements to credit spreads and bond prices. We use a version of this approach, which has been helpful. Conditional forecasting is also an area that's worth a look. In the asset-backed, CMBS, and mortgage markets, some exciting and productive modeling has been done and we have used it successfully. Lehman Brothers provides all-around very good fixed-income research. Salomon Analytics' The Yield Book Fixed-Income Analytical System (www.yieldbook.com) is another great source.

Question: Given that Lincoln Capital Management offers both enhanced-indexing and core-plus strategies, can you give us a sense of the fees you charge for such accounts and the expectations for added value and volatility?

Meyer: For a $100 million account, we start at about 10 bps for enhanced indexing and 7.5 bps for a passive portfolio. For a $500 million account, the numbers go down to 5 and 4 bps, respectively. We have an account for which the marginal fee is a single basis point. (We pray for slow growth in that account!) Enhanced indexing, when properly structured, offers a maximum return of, say, 15–25 bps over the benchmark with little downside risk (i.e., few quarters of return below the benchmark). This approach is quite different from core-plus, which may offer an expected return of 50 bps above the benchmark but may very likely expose the client's portfolio to an equal measure of downside risk.

Question: The Lehman Aggregate benchmark has 160 securities, which are intended to compensate for credit-specific risk, but if one credit goes under, a portfolio can still have a big exposure. Is there any way to address this problem through total-return swaps, even though they seem to be priced aggressively?

Meyer: There's no way to protect against credit-specific risk with total-return swaps. We conduct credit research that attempts to relate credit spreads and bond price movements to stock price movements, and we have nicknamed this approach "torpedo monitoring." It is simply a defensive mechanism dictating that when something smells bad, you should get out. But you do need to be careful about giving up too much yield. A consistent, higher-credit-quality portfolio will eventually create a persistent return deficiency. This torpedo monitoring, plus a strong diversification policy, is the best protection. We have taken our share of hits this year, but none has hurt.

Question: If you had an opportunity to start a new fixed-income firm, how would you structure it?

Meyer: I don't think competing in the index business is worthwhile because you can't compete with what is offered by firms such as ourselves, State Street Corporation, Barclays Global Investors, and Mellon Financial Corporation. You need to find a niche and excel in it. High-yield and distressed debt are good examples. Both are higher-fee and wider-margin businesses and are conducive to smaller firms. Managing corporates with a risk-control bias would certainly not be the worst idea that you could come up with right now. But it is very difficult to start a business today without outside financing. Everything I have discussed, such as quantitative research and model building, costs a lot of money. You can no longer do it on your own.

Credit: The New Source of Event Risk

Kathleen M. Shanley, CFA
Senior Corporate Bond Analyst
Gimme Credit, Inc.
Chicago

Because performance may be improved simply by avoiding credit disasters, analysts should not neglect the basic techniques of fundamental analysis. Although fraud and abuse may be difficult to detect, in the case of some recent financial scandals, analysts did not need to know every single detail in order to have reason to question the viability of the companies. The example of Comdisco demonstrates that thoughtful scrutiny of publicly available information can provide ample warning before catastrophe strikes.

In an increasingly volatile market environment, investment firms are combining fundamental analysis and modeling techniques, such as the approach used by Moody's KMV,[1] to enhance the overall performance of their bond portfolios. This presentation will focus on the fundamental analysis of specific securities and on the important role played by the rating agencies. Portfolio diversification is essential, but recent events, including the implosion of credits once viewed as stable (such as the Enron Corporation and WorldCom), suggest bondholders may be able to improve performance by minimizing exposure to credit "blowups."

I will discuss some reasons for the perceived financial schizophrenia of bonds versus equities, but I will also emphasize areas of common ground between bond and equity analysis. The goal in returning to basics in credit analysis is not to reject innovation but rather to blend fundamental analysis with quantitative modeling tools for maximum effect. Finally, I will conclude with a case study that suggests corporate bond analysts should have been able to identify red flags at the leasing company Comdisco well before the company's bankruptcy filing in 2001.

Complex Markets, Basic Methods

Dramatic changes have occurred within the corporate bond market in the past few years. Technological change roiled once-stodgy industries, such as telecommunications and utilities. A single-minded focus on shareholder value led some companies to increase leverage in order to fund share buybacks and speculative investments. The overall complexity of the capital markets increased as a result of the greater use of derivatives, structured finance, and off-balance-sheet funding vehicles. In many cases, new approaches helped reduce risk, but the complexity also made companies more difficult to analyze.

When equity markets were buoyant, it was easy even for start-up ventures to refinance maturing debt obligations in a "friendly" market, but once the Internet bubble burst, investors became risk averse. These factors converged to create the "fallen angels," whereby companies that were shut out of the capital markets slid rapidly from an investment-grade rating to a junk rating or even into default, often with little warning from the rating agencies. In the wake of this turmoil, bondholders are seeing lower recoveries on defaulted securities. According to Moody's Investors Service, the average recovery rate on defaulted bonds in 2001 slipped to a record low of 21 percent of par, sharply below the $41 per $100 average par-value recovery the rating agency estimated for the 1982–2001 period.

In the current environment, being a buy-and-hold investor is difficult. Investors need to continually monitor the securities in their portfolios. Although innovative modeling techniques, such as the KMV approach, can help, analysts should not neglect basic techniques of fundamental analysis: examining core earnings, liquidity, and financial flexibility; studying primary-source documents, such as U.S. SEC quarterly filings and debt prospectuses;

[1] Please see Mr. Kealhofer's presentation in this proceedings.

reading the footnotes; and doing the "detective" work to see if a company's fundamental trends live up to its press releases.

Analysts should be especially cautious of management "spin." In October 2000, the SEC adopted Regulation FD (Fair Disclosure), a set of rules aimed at barring issuers from selectively disclosing material nonpublic information. Since the implementation of Regulation FD, most companies are no longer whispering advance notice of earnings trends to favored analysts. They are more likely to hold conference calls that are made available to the general public via Webcasts. At the same time, some companies are tempted to use conference calls and analyst meetings as an opportunity to "spin" (i.e., to hype a version of corporate earnings trends that downplays unpleasant details). To a limited extent, such tactics are legitimate, but some extreme cases have occurred. For example, at insurer Conseco (which subsequently filed for bankruptcy in December 2002), CEO Gary Wendt put out a series of folksy "turnaround" memos about the "new" Conseco, yet virtually every quarter, the company's SEC filings would include negative disclosures that Wendt had not emphasized in his pronouncements.

The disclosure included in SEC filings may not always be as fully comprehensive as analysts would like, but these documents often contain significant information about funding and liquidity issues. Reviewing reams of SEC documents may sometimes be time-consuming, but these filings remain the best source for the fundamental data that analysts need to derive a credit opinion.

Rating Agencies and Triggers

Credit analysts cannot ignore the important role played by rating agencies in the corporate debt markets. Debate over the role of rating agencies heated up in 2002. The two primary agencies, Moody's Investors Service and Standard & Poor's (S&P), were accused alternately of responding too slowly or too precipitously to events in the corporate debt markets, particularly when a company teetered on the margin of an investment-grade rating. Various studies have shown that a clear correlation exists between credit ratings and the probability of default, but lags occur often enough to provide an incentive for analysts to try to anticipate rating agency actions and to sell vulnerable securities in advance of a potential downgrade.

Like other credit analysts, rating agencies rely primarily on publicly available financial data in evaluating an issuer. But unlike other analysts, rating agencies are considered to be corporate insiders, exempt from the requirements of Regulation FD. During the credit-rating process, rating agency analysts may receive various types of information not available to the public market, such as budgets and forecasts, as well as advance warning of pending financings, acquisitions, or restructurings. The rapid downfall of Enron, however, showed that rating agencies are sometimes no more successful than the public markets in ferreting out material information about credit trends.

Rating agencies play a unique role (potentially fraught with conflicts of interest) in the capital markets because they are paid by the rated debt issuers. They also have become pivotal in the world of structured finance, in which a rating from a rating agency is often a critical factor in influencing an investor's decision to buy various tranches of an asset-backed transaction.

In 2002, rating triggers became an increasingly important focus of concern. Overall, rating agencies perform a useful role in the capital markets, but the fact that debt issuers and investment bankers have put rating triggers into various types of agreements can exacerbate the significance of rating actions and turn the rating agencies into unwitting actors in financial dramas, as happened in 2001 with Enron. In extreme cases, a trigger intended to protect investors can instead set off a liquidity crisis by terminating credit facilities or requiring immediate repayment of obligations that would otherwise be repaid on a more leisurely schedule.

Both Moody's and S&P recently published studies examining the phenomenon of rating triggers.[2] In December 2001, Moody's surveyed nearly 1,900 U.S. nonfinancial corporate debt issuers. Of 771 responding companies with debt rated Ba1 or higher, 675 issuers reported a total of 2,819 rating triggers, with the potential to unleash 3,681 distinct effects. Only 635, or about 22 percent, of the triggers were publicly disclosed in SEC filings. This statistic is disturbing because the rating agencies factor triggers into their credit assessments but are not at liberty to disclose such details if companies themselves have not reported them publicly.

On closer examination, the Moody's report on triggers is somewhat less alarming because the most common triggers would not necessarily provoke a liquidity crunch. Survey respondents reported that the most frequently used triggers are collateral, letter

[2]Pamela M. Stumpp and Monica M. Coppola, "Moody's Analysis of U.S. Corporate Rating Triggers Heightens Need for Increased Disclosure," Special Comment, Moody's Investors Service (July 2002). Solomon B. Samson, "Identifying Ratings Triggers and Other Contingent Calls on Liquidity—Part 2," Standard & Poor's (15 May 2002).

of credit, and bonding provisions, all of which account for nearly 22 percent of the total. Typically, these provisions require a company to post a letter of credit, collateral, a surety bond, or some other form of enhancement in the event of a downgrade. These triggers are commonly used to ensure performance in derivatives contracts, commercial agreements, sale and leaseback arrangements, and accounts receivable securitizations.

The second most common trigger is a change in the pricing grid. About 21 percent of occurrences fall into this category. This version of a trigger attempts to link debt pricing with a company's credit risk. Such grids are routinely seen in loan agreements, although a large increase could affect a company's ability to meet its fixed charges.

Self-insurance accounted for about 12 percent of the triggers found by Moody's. Under these provisions, often found in lease agreements, if an issuer's rating is downgraded it is no longer permitted to self-insure its obligations and must instead purchase third-party insurance.

Termination-event provisions, typically found in swap agreements, account for 8.5 percent of the triggers reported to Moody's. If a company's rating is downgraded to below investment grade, it may be required to settle the swap. This type of trigger requires a cash payment only on out-of-the-money swap positions.

Moody's identified several triggers that can have a major impact on a company's liquidity: default, acceleration, and put triggers. These provisions account for few of the triggers on a percentage basis (default accounts for 5.3 percent; acceleration, 4.0 percent; and puts, 3.0 percent) but rank among the most serious. A company may be propelled unexpectedly into a liquidity crisis if it suddenly loses access to a line of credit or is forced to repay a large bond issue at a time when it may have limited access to the capital markets because of concerns about a downgrade. If companies were allowed more time to work out their funding problems, the impact might not be so severe.

The S&P survey reinforces Moody's findings. In early 2002, S&P surveyed about 1,000 U.S. and European investment-grade industrial and utility companies in order to examine their exposure to contingent calls on liquidity. The S&P survey focused on triggers with the potential to affect liquidity and excluded debt with pricing grids and event-risk covenants calling for a rate step-up. From this universe, S&P identified 24 "credit-cliff" companies, including the 15 U.S. issuers shown in **Exhibit 1**.

When S&P published its study in May 2002, it said any "current or imminent" concerns about liquidity were already factored into its current rating assessment for the credit-cliff issuers. Between May and mid-September 2002, however, 8 of the 15 issuers were either downgraded or put on watch for a possible downgrade. The data suggest that triggers, although not the only credit issue facing these companies, make it more difficult to manage liquidity and thus more risky for bondholders to hold these credits. The only name in Exhibit 1 that was removed

Exhibit 1. Fifteen "Credit-Cliff" Companies, as Identified by S&P

Company	Rating at 15 May 02	Rating at 20 Sep 02
Aquila	BBB/Watch negative	BBB–
Black Hills Corp.	BBB	BBB
Dominion Resources	BBB+	BBB+
Dynegy Inc.	BBB/Watch negative	B–/Watch negative
Georgia-Pacific Corp.	BBB–	BBB–/Watch negative
Halliburton Co.	A–/Watch negative	A–/Watch negative
Mirant Corp.	BBB–	BBB–
Petroleum Geo-Services ASA	BBB–/Watch negative	BB–
PG&E National Energy Group	BBB	BB+/Watch negative
Philadelphia Gas Works	BBB/Watch negative	BBB
Raytheon Co.	BBB–	BBB–
Reliant Resources Inc.	BBB/Watch negative	BB+/Watch negative
SEMCO Energy Inc.	BBB	BBB
Tyco International Ltd.	BBB/Watch developing	BBB–/Watch negative
The Williams Companies Inc.	BBB+/Watch negative	B+/Watch negative

Source: Based on data from Solomon B. Samson, "Identifying Ratings Triggers and Other Contingent Calls on Liquidity—Part 2," Standard & Poor's (15 May 2002).

from negative watch between May and September was Philadelphia Gas Works. In that instance, the company was able to negotiate the removal of a trigger in a letter of credit backing its commercial paper program.

Rating agencies are warning issuers that they will not withhold a downgrade if fundamentals warrant such a decision, even if the move will activate a trigger. Bond analysts need to be vigilant about triggers because they are not always fully disclosed or are disclosed only deep in appendixes of SEC filings or loan agreements. Although the S&P report identified only 24 companies on a credit cliff, others may emerge over time. Analysts need to evaluate the effect rating agency actions might have on the performance of a credit over time.

A recent example of the concerns raised by rating triggers is Americredit Corporation, a subprime auto lender facing questions about its financial flexibility. The company's 10-K for the fiscal year ended 30 June 2002 provides a mix of specific and open-ended disclosures that make an analysis of credit risk difficult. The 10-K filing makes the specific disclosure that in the event of a downgrade, certain derivative collateral lines will be reduced, requiring the company to pledge an additional $25 million to $40 million in cash. Analysts can use this statement to evaluate whether the potential exposure will be manageable. A vaguer statement in the 10-K is more ominous: "If the company's senior debt ratings are downgraded, then the lenders may require it to immediately repay all the outstanding debt under its facilities or may increase borrowing costs." Although appendixes attached to the 10-K provide more detail, the effect of additional downgrades on the company's financial prospects is unclear. Analysts need to keep pressuring companies to provide comprehensive disclosure and specifically identify all important triggers; otherwise, these provisions can have a sudden and unexpected negative impact on a company's prospects.

Financial Schizophrenia—Equities versus Bonds

Credit spreads and equity prices on occasion move in opposite directions but often follow the same trajectory. Credit analysts are more focused on downside risk, whereas equity analysts tend to emphasize growth. (Recently, equity analysts have begun to pay more attention to balance sheet and cash flow issues.) This is not to argue that credit analysts always do a better job of detecting problems. Certainly, cases have occurred in which bondholders were complacent because a large equity cushion seemed to support fixed obligations. In such instances, an earnings warning that suddenly drives down equity prices may have a corresponding negative effect on bond spreads.

Equity prices and bond spreads may diverge for a variety of reasons. Unlike bondholders, equityholders have an option on the upside. Corporate executives may take actions that favor equityholders over bondholders (at least in the short term), such as instituting a large share-repurchase program. A number of companies, particularly in cyclical industries, may now regret that they spent so much of their free cash flow on buybacks. Even equityholders are beginning to understand the need to maintain financial flexibility. Prudent financial policies can help maximize shareholder value in the long run.

I would not overstate the differences between good credit analysis and good equity analysis. Careful analysis that focuses on the balance sheet and on cash flow can provide early indications of problems and help both fixed-income and equity investors avoid costly mistakes. At the same time, the potential for stock price appreciation and the foundation for strong credit quality both ultimately depend on the ability of a company to generate earnings over time. For example, J.P. Morgan Chase & Company saw its stock drop sharply and its bond spreads widen in 2002. Its credit ratings fell (although only by one notch), even though it retained a significant capital base. Like equity investors, the rating agencies are concerned primarily with the eroding profitability of the bank's operations.

Both equity analysts and credit analysts are focusing more on the "core earnings" of a company's ongoing operations, which includes restructuring charges and write-downs of operating assets and excludes such items as goodwill impairment, litigation settlements, or asset sales. S&P recently proposed a standardized definition of core earnings.[3] Analysts are trying to pull back from some of the more extreme pro forma types of analysis that have made earnings trends look rosier than they really were.

Events of the past year show that liquidity is another issue of joint concern to equity investors and bondholders. Consider this industry comparison: In 2002, investment banking firms demonstrated good management of liquidity (even with stock prices down and capital markets weak) because the industry now understands that it must have the confidence of (and access to) the capital markets. In contrast, several energy companies that had no previous experience with market cycles (coming from a regulated

[3]David M. Blitzer, Robert E. Friedman, and Howard J. Silverblatt, "Measures of Corporate Earnings," Standard & Poor's (originally released 7 November 2001 and revised 14 May 2002).

utility environment) found themselves in a financial squeeze. The current economic environment demands that companies have a belt-and-suspenders mentality. It is not enough to have a commercial paper backup line, because tapping a backup line is interpreted by the market as a serious indication of financial vulnerability. Companies need to arrange a backup for the backup line, such as an asset-backed financing facility.

Disclosure Problems

Disclosure issues are another area of common ground for debt and equity analysts. Fraud is difficult to detect, but analysts did not need to know all the details of the abuses leading up to the rash of recent financial scandals in order to have raised questions about the financial strength of some fallen companies. Tyco International is a glaring example. Some analysts raised questions about Tyco's accounting and aggressive acquisitions years before the revelations of the past year. Although Enron hoodwinked nearly everyone from bankers and insurers to rating agencies, at least one prominent investor, Jim Chanos, contends that most of the company's problems were hidden in plain sight. Although some of the fraudulent activity may have been material, most of the large companies involved in recent scandals showed public signs of trouble well before any fraudulent behavior was disclosed. Analysts should not simply conclude that they had no responsibility for identifying problems sooner. For example, before fraud disclosures were ever made, WorldCom had already been downgraded and analysis of the company's financial statements indicated that its debt-protection measures had weakened.

Using fraud as an excuse for lack of responsibility is particularly unconvincing when it comes from such leading executives as William Harrison, CEO of J.P. Morgan Chase, who argued in a recent editorial in the *Wall Street Journal* that banks are actually victims in fraud cases.[4] I am suggesting not that investment banks were active arrangers of fraudulent accounting but that they were, in effect, enablers, facilitating the financing deals for irresponsible companies. Bankers should have been able to identify some of the problems, or potential problems, through good credit analysis.

The disclosure issue has become a fad, with companies suddenly racing to position themselves as leaders on corporate governance. Citigroup is one such company. CEO Sandy Weill recently described all that Citigroup is doing to improve its corporate governance, highlighting the company's independent board, its integrity in financial reporting, proper audit controls, adoption of the new SEC rules on timing (Citigroup plans to release its reports earlier than the SEC requirement mandates), expensing of employee stock options, and the decision to lower the assumed returns for pension accounting.

The open question about disclosure is whether all the public posturing of companies amounts to more than just window dressing. Citigroup and J.P. Morgan Chase and other companies may pledge to be leaders in corporate governance, but will the changes in disclosure be long lasting? The answer depends in large measure on analysts and investors continuing to pressure companies to provide better disclosure. Even if the disclosure is comprehensive, one could argue that some companies, such as Citigroup, are so large that even corporate insiders cannot know everything that goes on within the company or fully understand all the associated risks. Disclosure is fine, but corporate debt issuers also need to maintain the financial flexibility and liquidity that will help them weather a storm.

The Case of Comdisco

The history of leasing company Comdisco provides an interesting case study in fundamental credit analysis and serves as an example of how bond and equity analysts sometimes view the same company in different ways. In our case, we added Comdisco to our Gimme Credit Bottom Ten List at the same time that the stock's price was hitting its all-time high in March 2000. Comdisco's core business was leasing mainframe equipment. With the decline of that business, the company made a significant change in its strategy. The company's new management moved heavily into venture equity and the leasing of equipment to venture companies. It even had its own telecom start-up venture, and for a short time, its stock price reached stratospheric levels based on the euphoria over the venture equity gains, some of which were unrealized and some of which were cashed out but reinvested in the telecom start-up. With its strong BBB rating and history as a traditional leasing company, Comdisco continued to fund new and riskier investments largely with short-term debt. Its strategy depended on "friendly" capital markets because the company planned to issue a tracking stock for its venture investments and sell off or find partners for its telecom business. With the bursting of the Internet bubble, Comdisco's stock price fell quickly from its peak in March 2000, and its problems accelerated when the company conceded in October 2000 that it could not continue funding its telecom start-up. By

[4] "Banks Were Victims in Fraud Cases, Not Accomplices," *Wall Street Journal* (18 September 2002).

April 2001, Comdisco had to draw down its bank facilities and its rating was cut to junk. By July, it was bankrupt.

A credit analyst looking at Comdisco's balance sheet as of 31 March 2000 could easily have spotted several serious problems, as shown in **Table 1**. The company had drawn down its cash balance and had moved into riskier assets, such as venture equity securities. Property, plant, and equipment (PP&E) had risen dramatically because of the investment in the telecom start-up. Comdisco contended that its debt-to-equity measures were stable, as shown in **Table 2**, and actually had improved relative to the historical trend, which is probably one reason the rating agencies did not immediately downgrade the company. The reality, however, was that Comdisco had increased its debt burden, and although book equity had also increased, the increase was boosted by unrealized gains on venture investments. The company was able to realize some of the gains but poured the proceeds back into the failing telecom start-up. Other gains were unrealized, although shown on a mark-to-market basis on the balance sheet. The gains evaporated when the stock market began its steep decline.

Comdisco's troubles were compounded by the fact that so much of its debt was maturing within a short time frame, as shown in **Table 3**. Thus, when the company ran into problems in the market, it simultaneously faced resistance from bondholders, who were waking up to the company's situation and were unwilling to refinance Comdisco's debt.

To summarize, Comdisco's 31 March 2000 financial position raised multiple red flags that could have been detected by good credit analysis despite its record-high stock price. It also had other characteristics that should have drawn greater scrutiny from equity analysts, including an inexperienced management team and a sudden shift in business strategy. The telecom venture and related exit strategy depended completely on favorable capital market conditions. Such dependence has been a problem for many companies in the past few years. When capital markets shut down, a company that is highly dependent on access to new outside funds for continued survival will have a problem.

Table 1. Comdisco's Growth in High-Risk Assets (in US$ millions)

Assets	31 Mar 00	30 Sep 99	Change
Cash	$ 122	$ 407	–70%
Receivables	962	722	33
Leased assets	5,638	5,623	
Equity securities	636	252	152
PP&E	441	229	93
Other assets	616	574	
Total	$8,415	$7,807	

Source: Based on data from SEC filings and Gimme Credit.

Table 2. Comdisco's Leveraged Balance Sheet (in US$ millions)

Liabilities	31 Mar 00	30 Sep 99
Debt	$5,902	$5,571
Other liabilities	1,240	1,176
Equity	1,273	1,060
Total liabilities and equities	$8,415	$7,807
Debt/equity (×)	4.6	5.3

Source: Based on data from SEC filings and Gimme Credit.

Conclusion

Although analysts should avail themselves of new and sophisticated portfolio management tools, focusing on the fundamentals of a company remains critical in avoiding credit blowups. Analysts also need to understand the role of rating agencies and how triggers exacerbate the effect that rating actions can have on the creditworthiness of a company. Investors should continue to pressure companies to provide better disclosure so that analysts can make more-informed decisions about credit fundamentals.

Table 3. Comdisco's Reliance on Short-Term Debt (in US$ billions)

	2000	2001	2002	2003+	Total
Annual maturities at 30/9/99	$2.5	$1.0	$1.5	$0.6	$5.6
Percent of debt outstanding	45%	18%	27%	10%	100%

Source: Based on data from SEC filings (10-K for the fiscal year ended 30 September 1999) and Gimme Credit.

Question and Answer Session

Kathleen M. Shanley, CFA

Question: When meeting with management teams, what are the key questions you ask to determine if they are honest and creditworthy?

Shanley: As my colleague Carol Levenson always says, you have to remember that management members are not under oath in these forums or investor meetings. Although listening to what management has to say is important, analysts need to judge companies by what they do, not what they say. If management says having an A rating is important, do they act in ways to maintain the rating? Do they use equity as partial funding for acquisitions? Do they pay off debt when they say they will? Rather than simply accepting what companies have to say, analysts have to go back to the financial statements and examine the company's record. What did the company do in the previous cycle? What did management say in prior meetings and conference calls and was it consistent with what was disclosed in filings?

Question: Are there other red flags in the recent highly publicized fraud cases that analysts should be aware of?

Shanley: Yes. Analysts need to analyze the balance sheet and be aware of any sudden unexplained changes in receivables or inventory, but more broadly, they should be wary of companies with aggressive growth strategies. I worked with a credit manager whose motto was "if it grows like a weed, it's probably a weed." Occasionally, a high-growth start-up turns out to be a Wal-Mart or Microsoft, but more often, they turn out to be like Tyco. Be careful and ask questions about where all the growth is coming from.

Question: A company's bank credit lines are more important than ever. What determines whether a company needs to disclose the details of its bank lines in its SEC filings?

Shanley: As an analyst, I like to know about the bank credit lines and think they should always be disclosed. Rating agencies are also starting to emphasize the importance of disclosure in this area. For example, in 2002, Moody's published a liquidity assessment that flags such issues as the existence of material-adverse-change (MAC) clauses in credit lines. If a company has a MAC clause in a bank line, analysts need to know about it or any other kind of trigger related to ratings. Again, analysts have to look at how much a company is relying on bank credit for its operations.

Question: Have bond buyers been lax in requiring collateral, triggers, or assurances to enhance our positions as lenders vis-à-vis the banks, and what can we do to change?

Shanley: The issue is complicated. If you own a security that has a trigger, activation of the trigger could lead to a default for the company, in which case you are not necessarily any better off. A few years ago, when times were good, the only choice was to buy or not to buy. These days, if you don't feel like you have the protection you need, you need to step back and not buy. If enough people step back, it will influence the spread that the issuer can command or the covenants it will have to offer.

Question: Given that the latest loan officer survey indicates a lack of credit demand from corporations, are we in a credit crunch?

Shanley: We're in a two-track world. Companies that have reasonably good credit fundamentals are not experiencing a credit crunch. Certainly, the bond market has seen plenty of new issuance, with good receptivity for the stronger names. Companies with problematic credit fundamentals are probably having trouble obtaining funding at any price, but it is also true that overall demand is weak.

Question: What beaten-down sectors or individual credits are of value in the current market?

Shanley: We tend to focus mainly on individual credits rather than particular sectors. Obviously, many names that have survived this market are trading at amazingly wide spread levels. But is all the bad news out? These things seem to be taking a long time to work through. I mainly follow the financial sectors, and I've recently tended to favor some of the regional banks. I've also recommended Citigroup. Citigroup shares the same headline and litigation risk as J.P. Morgan Chase, but it also has tremendous cash flow. You have to look at the earnings power of big names. For example, Bank of America has a lot of credit exposure, but it also has a national franchise.

Question: What number of credits or companies (within industries/sectors) is reasonable to cover in depth, and is there more value in looking at credits that are on the cusp when trying to pick winners and avoid losers?

Shanley: Ideally, at Gimme Credit, we would like to have enough analysts that one analyst could cover just a small sector of the market. In reality, I cover 75 or more names. I try to look for those companies that are changing their model, taking on new risks, and taking on a lot of event risk. Analysts have to maximize their time by focusing on the smaller percentage of names that are likely to become a problem.

Question: Please comment on the divergence of General Electric Company's (GE's) stock price and credit rating (i.e., the stock price has fallen 50 percent but the credit rating remains the same).

Shanley: Bondholders awoke to some of the risks of holding GE debt in 2002. William Gross of PIMCO had a widely publicized debate with GE about its amount of short-term debt, the lack of support by backup credit lines, and some large potential rating-trigger exposure that was disclosed in its most recent 10-K. In response to pressure from Gross and other fixed-income investors, the company has made some changes and is adding more bondholder protections, which are positive developments. GE still has disclosure issues, but I nevertheless view it as a high-quality company.

Portfolio Management of Credit Risk

Stephen Kealhofer
Managing Director
Moody's KMV
San Francisco

Although the Sharpe–Markowitz framework developed for equity portfolio management can be applied to debt portfolios, doing so can lead to strange conclusions, such as unacceptably large credit concentrations. One possible solution is to combine the Sharpe–Markowitz approach with the Merton–Black–Scholes framework. This alternative method offers a valuable tool for analyzing stand-alone default probabilities and portfolio risk contributions, optimizing risk and return, and analyzing portfolios to attribute performance *ex post*.

KMV has been providing portfolio analysis tools for credit risk for about nine years. The fourth generation of these models has provided useful insights into portfolio management issues, particularly diversification.[1] This presentation offers a brief review of our approach to credit risk and a discussion of how it can be applied to portfolio management, benchmarking, and performance attribution. Our portfolio approach is based on the work of Harry Markowitz and Bill Sharpe. Although the approach they developed for portfolio analysis is usually applied to equity portfolios, it can also be applied to debt portfolios. Many of the insights gained from working with equities, however, do not naturally flow to the analysis of debt. For example, one issue confronting the asset management world is that fixed-income benchmarks imply credit concentrations that no investor would want to hold, such as 7 percent in Ford Motor Company or 2.5 percent in WorldCom. KMV's quantitative approach melds the Sharpe–Markowitz portfolio approach with the option-theoretic credit modeling of the Merton–Black–Scholes approach. These conceptual frameworks are useful because they tell us how to use the available price data coming out of markets to make real-world portfolio decisions. In addition to the information from equity markets, we incorporate data from the bond and credit derivatives markets. As activity in these markets has increased in the past five years, so have the opportunities to gather information from them.

Basic Approach

KMV's original work was targeted primarily at commercial banks following the 1990–91 recession, but beginning in the mid-1990s, we began to add insurance companies and asset managers to our client base. This orientation allows us to track credit issues quite extensively. Using market data from more than 40 countries, including many in which we have a client base, we currently follow approximately 25,000 companies on a daily basis.

Applying the Merton Model. Our approach is largely based on the credit risk analysis developed by Robert Merton.[2] Our basic measure of the default risk of a company is driven by three variables: the value of liabilities, the value of assets, and the volatility of asset values. Other variables enter the analysis that are beyond the scope of this presentation, such as how much a company is paying in dividends and the optionality in its liabilities, but these three variables are the primary drivers. Their relationships are illustrated in **Figure 1**. The y-axis measures the market value of the entire company, not just the company's equity component. The x-axis denotes the passage of

[1] I cofounded KMV in 1989 with John Andrew McQuown and Oldrich Alfons Vasicek. In the spring of 2002, KMV was acquired by Moody's Corporation, but as a separate operating subsidiary of Moody's it will continue with its previous business plan.

[2] See, for example, Robert C. Merton, "On the Pricing of Corporate Debt: The Risk Structure of Interest Rates," *Journal of Finance* (May 1974):449–470.

Figure 1. The Merton Model: Risky Assets and the Probability of Default

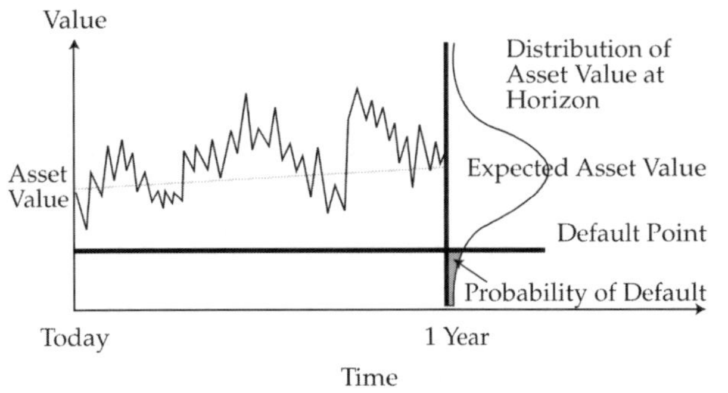

time. The company has a known market value today (which can be deduced by a method that will be discussed shortly), but that value can be expected to change over time. Although the future market value of a company's assets is unknown, on average, that future value will not differ much from the current value. This is true because in financial markets, if the expected value of an asset is significantly more or less than its current value, the buyers and sellers in the market will cause the current value to adjust to the expected value. Current values always reflect future expectations.

From a credit standpoint, the most important attribute is the volatility of future asset values or, put another way, the range of possible future asset values. We measure this both historically and by comparison with other companies with similar attributes. Much of a credit officer's subjective knowledge of credit is intuition about company volatilities. With the Merton approach, we can directly measure these volatilities. Finally, to complete this picture, we add what we call the "default point," which is based on the liabilities of the company. We have found that when the market value of the assets of a company falls to about 75 percent of the company's liabilities, the company defaults.

From an *ex ante* perspective, we can establish what the market value of assets is today and how far the market value will have to fall to reach the default point. We then express the size of that loss in terms of volatility. For example, if a company's asset value has to fall 80 percent to get to the default point and those assets have a volatility of 20 percent, the company is four standard deviations from its default point. We call this measure the "distance to default."

We use this information to assess the likelihood of the asset value falling to or below the default point. We do this by measuring the empirical probability of default, historically, for companies that were four standard deviations from the default point. When we consider the entire range of these empirical default frequencies, we find that the distribution is considerably more fat-tailed than a normal distribution. For instance, at four standard deviations, the normal distribution would indicate that the likelihood of default is about one-third of one-hundredth of a percent or 0.0033 percent, whereas we have empirically estimated the likelihood of default at six-tenths of a percent or 0.60 percent, a level of risk that is two orders of magnitude higher.

Estimating Market Value. Book or accounting value does not help in determining a company's worth. Instead, working from the liability side, we rely on two key insights from others. One, from Modigliani and Miller, says that the market value of a company's assets is equal to the market value of its fixed liabilities plus the market value of its equity.[3] This insight is useful, but it cannot really be operationalized because many liabilities do not have market values.

The second key insight, which originated with Black and Scholes[4] and was further developed by Merton,[5] says that the equity of a company is equivalent to a call option on the market value of the company's assets. The market value of that call option (the company's market capitalization) and the strike price and maturity of the option (how much the company owes and when) can be observed. This means that the market value of equity is functionally related to the market value of its assets, the volatility of those assets, the book value of its liabilities, and the value of those liabilities.

The value and volatility of equity can be expressed as a set of different equations of the same variables. Two equations and two unknowns result:

$$E = f[A, \sigma_A, \text{liability structure}]$$

and

$$\sigma_E = g[A, \sigma_A, \text{liability structure}],$$

where E is the market value of equity, σ_E is the volatility of equity value, A is the market value of assets, σ_A is the volatility of asset value, and the liability structure includes information about the size and maturities of fixed obligations. In options theory, the underlying asset characteristics are known and the option (equity) characteristics are derived. In the

[3]Franco Modigliani and Merton H. Miller, "The Cost of Capital, Corporation Finance, and the Theory of Investment," *American Economic Review* (June 1958):261–297.
[4]Fischer Black and Myron Scholes, "The Pricing of Options and Corporate Liabilities," *Journal of Political Economy* (May 1973):637–659.
[5]Robert C. Merton, "On the Pricing of Corporate Debt: The Risk Structure of Interest Rates," *Journal of Finance* (May 1974):449–470.

credit application, the option (equity) characteristics are known and the underlying asset characteristics are derived. Because we have two equations and two unknowns, this system can be solved.

Once asset value and volatility are estimated, we arrive at the default point by comparing that information with the liabilities of the company and determining the default point at a particular point in the future. As mentioned previously, this method enables us to summarize a company's credit risk in a measure we call "distance to default." The distance to default (DD_H) for a given horizon (H) can be expressed as a function of the current asset value (A_0), the default point at that horizon (X_H), which is based on the liability structure and the volatility of assets, or:

$$\mathrm{DD}(H) = \frac{\ln(A_0/X_H) + \text{"drift"}}{\sigma_A H}.$$

The cumulative probability of default or expected default frequency for the horizon (EDF_H) is an empirical function of the distance to default, or:

$\mathrm{EDF}(H)$ is approximately equal to $g[\mathrm{DD}(H)]$.

As I mentioned previously, the expected default frequency (EDF) function comes from an empirical mapping of distance to default (DD) to actual default experience. To implement this model, we track the default experience of all public companies in the United States back to 1973. In the past few years, we have also been collecting default data in other jurisdictions, mostly in Europe and the United Kingdom and, to a limited extent, in Australia and Asia.

Company Example. Consider the case of Comdisco, whose changing capital structure over time is shown in Panel A of **Figure 2**.[6] In our analysis, we look at the relationship between the market value of assets and the default point and take into account the volatility of Comdisco's assets. Panel B of Figure 2 shows the market value of assets and the default point on a log scale, along with the volatility of assets and the EDF measured on a percentage (annualized) basis. In our distance-to-default and EDF measures, the log difference is the numerator and the volatility of assets scaled for time is the denominator.

Interestingly, as Panel B indicates, the volatility of Comdisco's assets was relatively stable and then began rising until it more than doubled by early 2000. This asset volatility shift is dramatic and uncommon. Most companies have essentially the same asset volatility over a 5- or 10-year period. Even though equity volatilities may fluctuate considerably, the underlying asset volatilities do not. Such a large asset volatility shift was a significant indication that a major change in business activities was occurring at the company. In mid-1998, Comdisco's default probability was running at about 0.1 percent, which has been typical of A rated companies. Beginning in late 1998, it increased into the BBB range, and by early 2000, it entered the BB range—just as Comdisco's stock peaked in value.

We have found that when one accounts for asset volatility and market value, the picture is quite different from when equity values alone are considered. One of the characteristics of the recent tech "bubble" is that along with the very high multiples, we saw concomitant increases in asset volatility. It was as if the market was simultaneously signaling that the increased valuations were highly speculative. As a result, even though many of these companies had very large market values, their volatilities meant that they also had significant credit risk, even with quite low levels of liabilities. In other words, they had virtually no debt capacity despite their large market caps. If volatility is 50 percent a year, a two-standard-deviation event can wipe out a company.

Panel C of Figure 2 shows Comdisco's EDF against its Standard & Poor's (S&P) ratings. (Moody's would show about the same ratings, but S&P has made their data more easily available to us than has Moody's.) Comdisco's rating remained at BBB+ until its EDF had fallen into the B range. Such cases are not uncommon. Rating agencies have been caught in a vise between investors who expect the ratings to follow the fate of the corporations in an accurate and timely way and investors who are adversely affected by the decision to downgrade, particularly when the downgrade moves the company out of investment grade.

Portfolio Analysis

Our approach to credit risk gives us a blueprint for managing portfolios in a quantitative way. Modern portfolio theory, developed by Harry Markowitz[7] in the 1950s and later elaborated by William Sharpe[8] and many others, is only partially suited to the analysis of credit risk because it was designed for assets that have more bell-shaped payoff distributions. When we apply it to credit risk, we have to constantly bear in mind that such measures as standard deviation and variance can be misleading when the underlying asset value distributions are non-normal.

[6]For further discussion of Comdisco, please see Ms. Shanley's presentation in this proceedings.

[7]Harry M. Markowitz, "Portfolio Selection," *Journal of Finance* (March 1952):77–91.

[8]William F. Sharpe, "Capital Asset Prices: A Theory of Market Equilibrium under Conditions of Risk," *Journal of Finance* (September 1964):425–442.

Figure 2. Comdisco Fundamentals, September 1996–September 2001

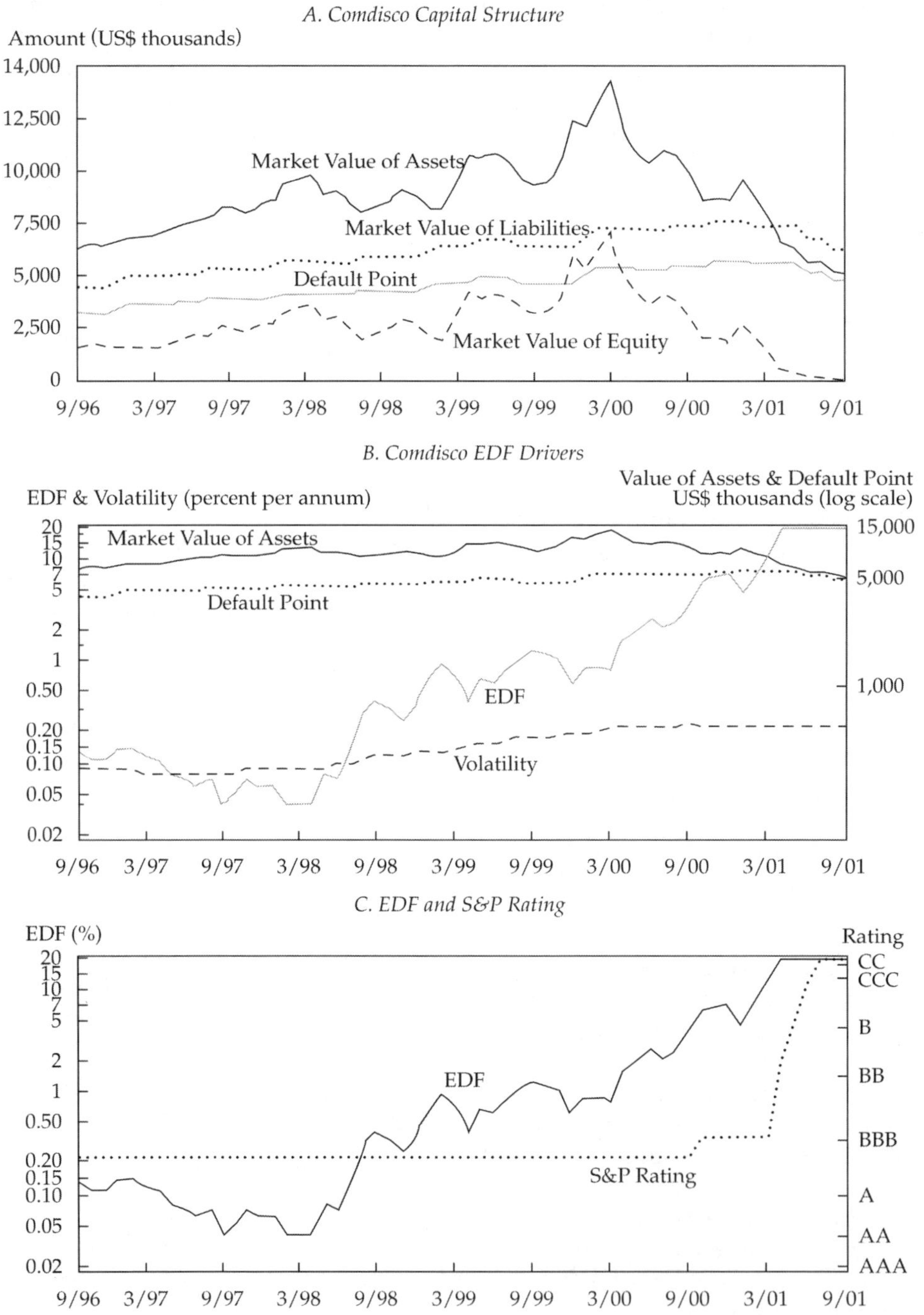

Note: EDF = expected default frequency.

Even though this framework was developed with equity portfolios in mind, applying it to equities in actual practice is difficult. Good measures of equity risk are obtainable, but good measures of equity expected return are not.

The reverse problem occurs when dealing with debt portfolios. Coming up with a good return expectation is not a problem. What companies have contracted to pay investors is known. We can then adjust that for the time value of money, optionality, and so on. In the KMV model, once we know the default probability, we can plug in reasonable numbers for expected recovery and adjust the spreads to what we call "expected spreads" to arrive at a good return expectation.

The problem in credit analysis is determining appropriate measures of risk. Three components are necessary for measuring portfolio risk: the expected return and stand-alone risk of each bond and a correlation for each pair of bonds. We just discussed the ease of expected return estimation, and quantifying the EDF enables us to estimate stand-alone risk. The more difficult question is estimating the correlations.

Credit risk is a function of the market value of assets, asset volatility, and the default point. Because the key to the relationship between two companies over time is the market value of their assets, if we understand how the market value of assets is correlated for two companies, we can use our analytical framework to deduce how their credit risks are correlated. At KMV, when we started examining credit risk about 16 years ago, we first began by calculating default correlations from historical data but quickly recognized the drawbacks of this approach. For example, what is the default correlation of Cisco Systems and Apple Computer? Their historical experience of default is completely unrevealing; we cannot derive a pairwise historical measure of their default risk because neither has experienced default.

The next approach we took was to compare entire industries, finding, for example, the correlation of default rates between computer manufacturers and telephone companies. (In the past, not many default rates in telephone companies were available, but now this industry supplies us with a rich data sample.) Detailed analysis, however, shows that the correlations measured on an industry basis are extremely noisy. To illustrate this, years ago we tried analyzing default rates in different Federal Reserve districts and the results were almost humorous. For example, our findings indicated that we should short Arkansas and go long Minnesota, which makes no sense. We quickly determined that the errors from using this process exceeded 100 percent and that the Merton structure offered a better way to calculate the default correlation—the first step being to understand the correlation of asset values and the second step to analytically deduce the default correlation from the asset value correlation.

Figure 3 depicts the joint default frequency for two companies, X and Y. This figure is like a topographical map, so imagine the concentric circles as a hill, with the top of the hill being the smallest oval. If we take a horizontal slice, we see the distribution of Company X's asset values, given certain values for Company Y's assets. Similarly, if we take a vertical slice, we see the distribution of Company Y's asset values, given certain values for Company X's assets. Each vertical or horizontal slice will be different because the two companies' asset values depend on one another; that is, they are jointly distributed. Joint distributions typically appear as ridges. The ridge conveys information about the way that the two companies' asset values are correlated. In practice, the correlations are always positive and the ridge is oriented along the positive 45-degree line. The only question is the magnitude of the correlation. The greater the correlation, the more narrow the ridge and the greater the likelihood of getting either two large values or two small values at the same time. The rounder the hill, the lower the correlation.

Figure 3. Joint Default Frequency for Two Companies

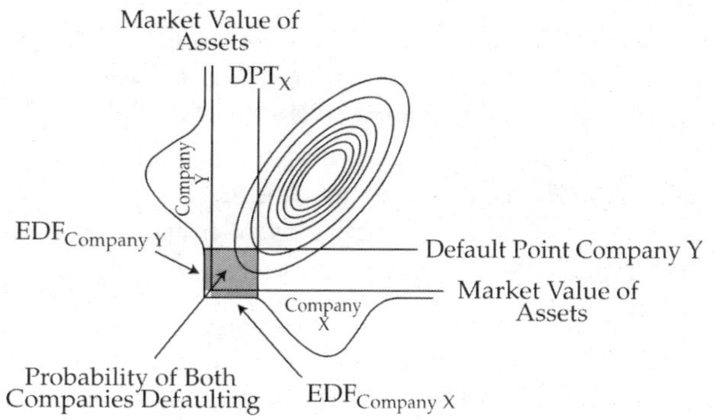

In effect, Figure 3 resembles a ("squashed") bell-shaped distribution in three dimensions. If we select a particular asset value for Company X and one for Company Y, the volume or area under the lower-left part of the hill starting at these values represents the likelihood that the asset value of Company X will be less than or equal to the selected value at the same time that the asset value of Company Y is less than or equal to the selected value.

In Figure 3, the default points (the asset values at which each company would default) have been added. So, following our earlier discussion, the joint probability of default is given by the volume under the lower-left quadrant of the hill starting at the two default points. In fact, Figure 3 provides a two-by-two classification table: the region where neither defaults, the region where both default, and the two regions where one defaults and the other does not. With such a mapping, all the necessary correlation information about credit risk can be deduced from the joint asset value distribution and from knowing the liability structure of each company.

Portfolio Management of Credit Risk

Once we have measured expected default frequencies, correlations, and exposure characteristics for the individual exposures, we can determine the portfolio distribution, measure diversification effects, and determine the risk–return trade-off.

Consider how a large portfolio appears using KMV's portfolio management software, as shown in Panel A of **Figure 4**. Each square represents an individual exposure. The vertical axis shows the asset's expected spread over the risk-free rate, reduced by the asset's expected loss. The expected loss is the EDF times what we would expect to lose if default occurred (the "loss given default," or LGD). The expected spread is what we are getting paid, on average, for taking the asset's credit risk. The horizontal axis shows the stand-alone risk of the asset. In

Figure 4. Portfolio Risk–Return Exposures

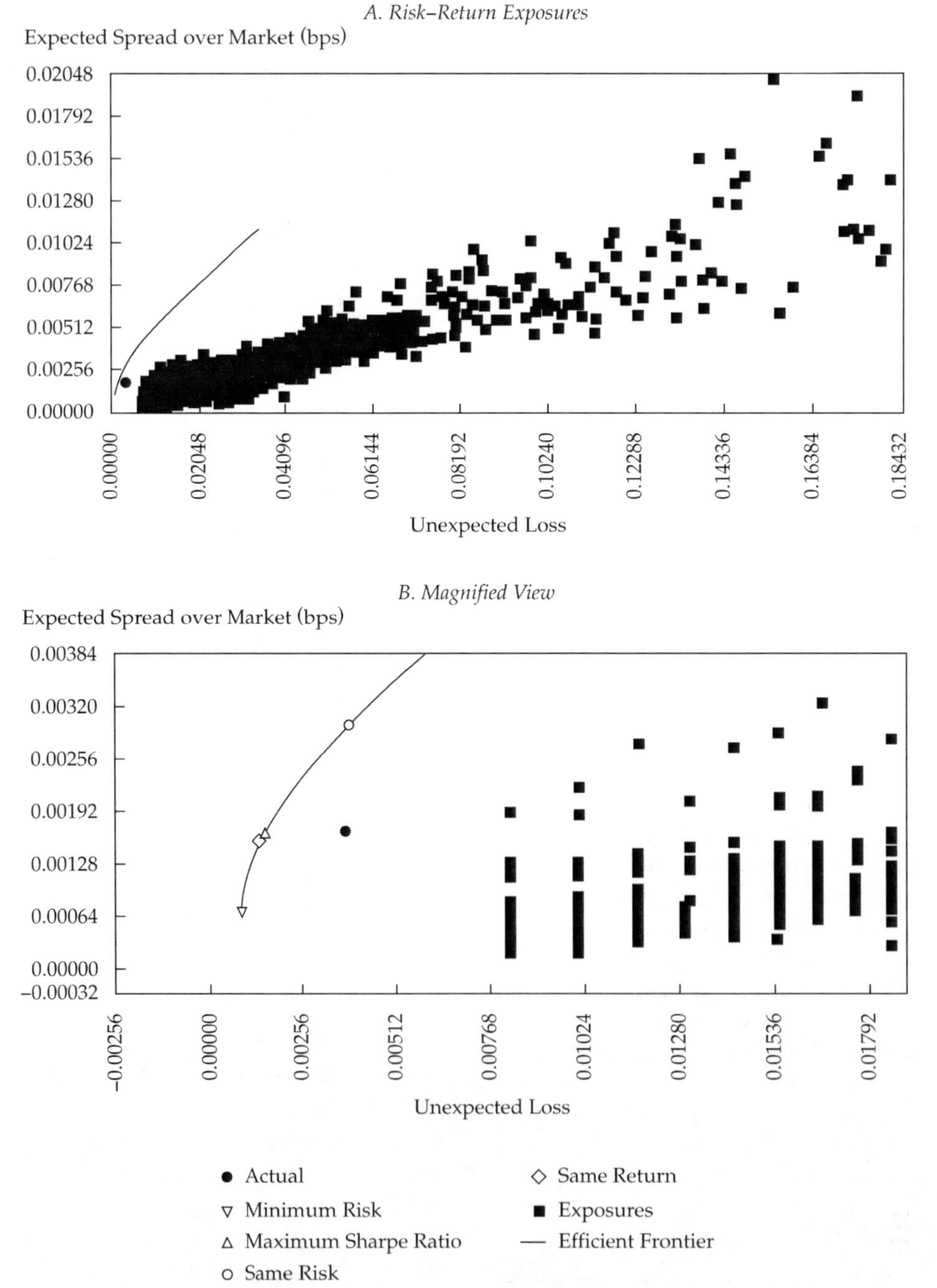

this case, risk is the standard deviation of future value—but only the portion attributable to the credit risk. So, the squares represent the stand-alone risk–return characteristics for all the individual assets in the portfolio.

The risk–return characteristics of the portfolio are represented by the circle at the lower left. The solid line, which depicts the efficient frontier for this set of individual exposures, indicates the maximum return level that is achievable for each level of risk. Panel B of Figure 4 offers a close-up view of the same portfolio. It shows that the risk of the portfolio is significantly less than even the lowest risk asset in the portfolio. Substantial diversification benefits can clearly be obtained in credit portfolios. In addition, Panel B of Figure 4 shows that the actual portfolio is off the efficient frontier. In this case, simply reweighting this portfolio can reduce risk by one-third without diminishing return, which is a typical outcome in analyzing real-world portfolios. We can usually achieve risk reductions of 25–50 percent by reweighting existing portfolios because most of the risk in a portfolio comes from a relatively small fraction of its assets. In many cases, 40 percent of risk in the portfolio comes from 5 percent of the holdings by market value. This characteristic distinguishes debt portfolios from equity portfolios.

Incidentally, the distributions of payoffs associated with these portfolios are highly non-normal. They have fat, long tails on the downside, indicating higher probabilities of negative outcomes than would be suggested by a normal distribution. We can use more-advanced methods than those of Markowitz to obtain a good measure of the probability of realizing any particular downside payoffs. **Figure 5** shows the value distribution for two portfolios, an actual portfolio that was analyzed and its optimized counterpart that has the same expected return but the maximum possible Sharpe ratio. Optimization in this case reduces risk by about one-third and substantially reduces the probability of downside events.

Managers build portfolios asset by asset. Thus, they need to make a judgment about how the addition or deletion of an individual asset is likely to affect overall portfolio risk. The key measure of this is the asset's "risk contribution."

Figure 4 demonstrates that the risk of the whole portfolio is substantially less than the risk of the least risky asset in it. That is, if we measure the weighted average of the risks of the assets in the portfolio, it would be much higher than the actual portfolio risk. Much of the risk of each individual asset is diversified away in the context of the portfolio—but not all of it. Some fraction remains, and the fraction depends on

Figure 5. Value Distribution: Actual Portfolio versus Optimized Portfolio

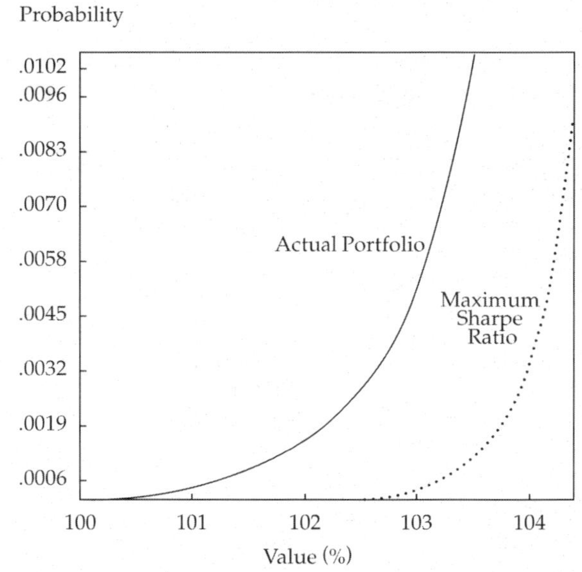

the stand-alone risk of the asset, how correlated it is with other assets in the portfolio, and the size of the exposure. The manager typically has control over only one of these factors—the amount of the asset held in the portfolio. Consequently, managers can change the risk contribution of an asset—its residual risk in the portfolio—by changing its weighting in the portfolio.

Figure 6 illustrates the return-to-risk characteristics of all assets in the portfolio. As in Figure 4, the expected spread is shown on the y-axis, but in Figure 6, the x-axis shows not the stand-alone risk but the amount of risk the individual asset contributes to the portfolio after taking into account diversification. We call this the asset's "risk contribution." A line drawn from the origin to any particular asset indicates the return-to-risk ratio for that asset in the context of the given portfolio. The squares represent assets that have approximately the same return-to-risk ratio as the portfolio as a whole. The circles represent assets that have positive portfolio performance with above-average return-to-risk ratios. The diamonds and triangles represent assets with negative return-to-risk ratios—the assets hurting overall performance.

Figure 6 indicates that most assets are helping overall portfolio performance and only a few are pulling it down. In general, a manager needs to scrutinize assets that are yielding too little return for the risk they add. Reducing holdings of low return-to-risk assets and increasing holdings of high return-to-risk assets raises the portfolio's overall return to risk.

Figure 6. Asset Returns and Risk Contributions: Beneficial and Detrimental Contributions

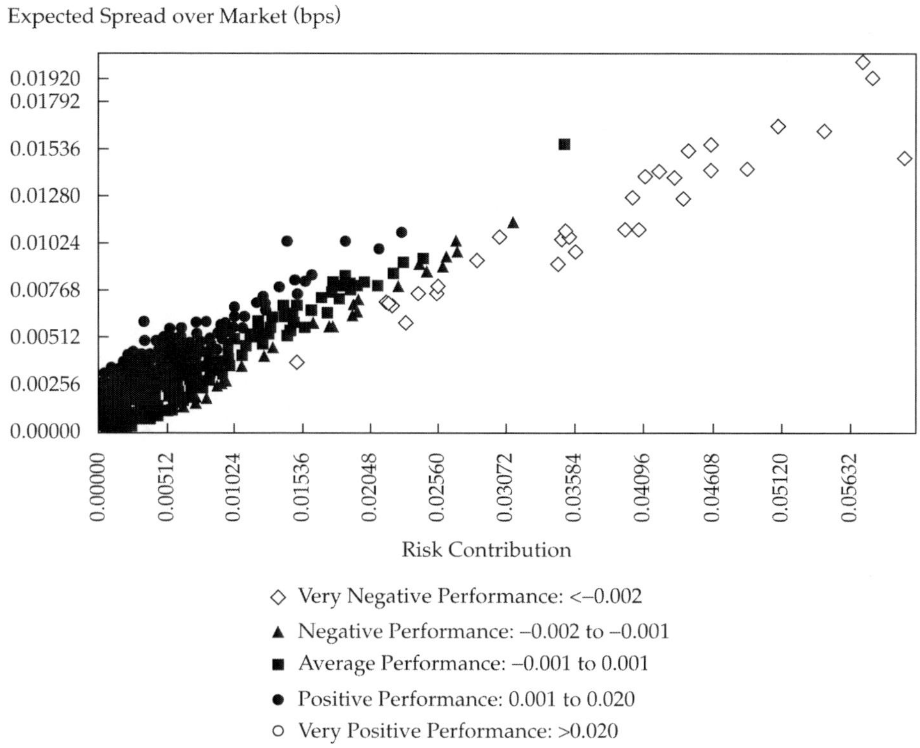

Portfolio Optimization

Several stylized facts can be deduced from our work. First, credit portfolios contain a wider range of risks than equity portfolios. Even though most investors think in terms of safe versus risky stocks and how they differ, the truth is that between the least risky stock and the most risky stock, the difference in risk is only about a factor of five. In contrast, in fixed-income portfolios we can almost always find an asset that is 200 times (and sometimes 1,000 times) riskier than the least risky asset. With equities, correlation is the primary driver determining optimal portfolio weights. With credit risk, because the risk differentials are so great, one of the key drivers is the standalone risk of each asset.

With credit portfolios, not only can a small number of assets contribute a large fraction of the total portfolio risk, but idiosyncratic risk is hard to eliminate. In short, debt portfolios are underdiversified. The rules of thumb used by people for equity analysis do not apply for fixed-income analysis. In equity, extremely large portfolios of 500–1,000 assets with attendant diversification benefits are common. In fixed income, managers continue to run extremely small portfolios with only 60–100 assets, even though diversification could be boosted substantially by increasing the number of assets. The practical difficulties notwithstanding, our analysis indicates that too much idiosyncratic risk exists in credit portfolios. Diversification yields a bigger payoff in credit than in equities, so fixed-income managers should hold substantially larger portfolios in terms of the number of assets than they typically do.

Benchmarking and Performance Attribution

Using the portfolio analysis I have described, managers can examine the issue of benchmarks. At KMV, a lengthy study of market-cap credit benchmarks found that the benchmarks are not even approximately optimal. An interesting conundrum arises: Any asset in excess of 1 percent in a portfolio is probably too much, yet the existing benchmarks encourage managers to hold much larger positions.

Our analysis also allows for examining the returns associated with the portfolio *ex post*. The default probabilities can be tied to the bond valuations quite well by using an option-pricing framework. In our work with valuation issues in bonds and other credit-sensitive instruments, we have found that the default probabilities we estimate using equity market values correspond quite well to the values we see in credit markets. We can implement a straightforward option-pricing framework by estimating one pricing parameter on a marketwide basis and can explain in excess of 70 percent of the cross-sectional variation in bond prices (and somewhat more once we start accounting for differences in recovery values). In other words, we can dissect portfolio performance and identify its drivers. Because default probabilities are primarily a function of asset value and volatility, we can break down that analysis to fundamentals by industry, country, and other segments, mimicking what has been done in equity analysis in the past.

Conclusion

KMV's approach, which has its basis in Merton's work of about 30 years ago, provides a powerful analytic framework for analyzing a variety of credit risk issues, such as stand-alone default probabilities and portfolio risk contributions. Furthermore, analytical portfolio management enables managers to optimize risk and return. The framework underlying KMV's models also gives managers the ability to monitor the return-to-risk profile of portfolios to determine appropriate comparative benchmarks for portfolios and to attribute performance *ex post*.

Question and Answer Session

Stephen Kealhofer

Question: Can KMV's techniques and tools be used to replicate the risk-and-return profile of the Lehman Aggregate Bond Index or another credit benchmark by using fewer issuers?

Kealhofer: You can dissect the Lehman Aggregate or any index and understand its credit components, so to a certain extent, it can be replicated. The problem is the idiosyncratic risk. You cannot replicate the idiosyncratic risk unless you match some of the particularly odd index weightings. As a practical matter, even though replication may be your mandate, you would be better off matching the systemic risk and trying to eliminate the idiosyncratic risk component.

Question: Has the effectiveness of KMV's methodology been evaluated for financial firms?

Kealhofer: More questions have arisen about financial firms than about nonfinancial firms. Our model's biggest perceived problem with financial firms has been that it shows significantly higher default probabilities for firms such as Morgan Stanley Dean Witter and Goldman Sachs than their debt ratings indicate. Across the financial sector as a whole, however, a good correspondence exists between our EDFs and the spreads that they imply and the spreads at which the firms' credits actually trade. Further, the performance of the model for financial firms has been rather timely in identifying all of the banks and other financial firms that have gotten into trouble, so I'm happy with it.

Question: How do you separate the signal from the noise in the KMV model?

Kealhofer: We take the market prices that we use in the models seriously. We don't dampen or filter them or add any subjective analysis. I don't view equity prices as having a noise component, because that would imply that I need to "fix" them in some way. With market prices, you need to try to understand the information that's reflected in them. You can choose to disagree with that information, but from my standpoint, my job is to accurately report the information that is in the market price. I leave it up to my clients to determine how much they want to rely on that information. The noise I'm concerned about is how well we measure the volatilities. Any volatility measure has some estimation error or "noise," and option approaches such as ours are sensitive to the input volatilities. About 70 percent of our research is devoted to how to measure volatility with minimal "noise."

Question: In your model, do you consider the maturity schedule for the debt?

Kealhofer: Yes, in the calculation of the default point, we pay attention to the maturity structure of the debt. Generally, we find that the shorter the maturity structure of the debt, the higher the default point and the higher the EDF. As we look at longer horizons, we increase the default point to contain a higher fraction of the long-term liabilities.

Question: When you develop your default correlation statistics, how do you deal with the fact that correlation statistics tend to spike up in difficult economic environments at the time when high correlations will do the most harm?

Kealhofer: The spiking of correlations is a measurement issue. If you divide the return for a company's debt into idiosyncratic and systemic components (i.e., independent factors and factors that it shares with other companies), the idiosyncratic components appear all the time and, by their nature, are unrelated to other companies. Periodically, such as when you have a crisis, the systemic components surface. So, when you measure correlation *ex post*, you see long periods of low correlation and short, infrequent periods of high correlation. From a correlation standpoint, you're trying to assess *ex ante* the likelihood of the systemic components surfacing and their magnitude relative to the nonsystemic components. What you want is a good *ex ante* measure of the likely frequency of crisis and noncrisis events, which is what correlation really measures.

In portfolio analysis, the distribution of future portfolio value that you're calculating indicates what happens when those crisis events show up. If the relative frequencies are correct in your correlations, then you have the right probabilities associated with the extreme events. In other words, you are correctly determining the future portfolio value distributions.

Question: What is the problem with debt indexes?

Kealhofer: The fundamental issue is that market-cap weights in credit have a number of unappealing features. Credit resembles an option. Consider how strange it would be to run a portfolio that reflected the market value of all the outstanding long call options in the stock market at any given time. The portfolio would be too heavily weighted toward certain names at any given time.

We've created a specialty in fixed-income management that invests only in bonds. From a conceptual standpoint, the bond universe doesn't make sense as an investment product. The market-cap weights are too large in a lot of names. If you dig into those names, these heavy weights are carrying big portfolios of credit and financing that credit in the commercial paper and debt markets. In this case, directly investing in the names in Ford's credit portfolios, for example, would be better than having to have so much exposure to Ford itself.

Narrowing the universe to the high-grade or high-yield U.S. fixed-income world puts too many constraints on the universe. Managers get corralled into these constrained universes by their benchmark mandates. The only solution is to break some of these binding, large-scale, institutional constraints. Otherwise, the type of credit performance managers can extract from portfolios will not be good and we will repeat the poor performance we've just seen. In particular, it probably does not make sense to separate high grade and high yield. You can construct a better portfolio using both universes together than by having to construct a portfolio from just one or the other. And that would mean that you would not need to buy or sell just because a credit moves across the boundary between the two. Who does that help, the dealer or the investor?

Question: Is the default point equal to, greater than, or less than the bankruptcy point?

Kealhofer: We don't distinguish a separate bankruptcy point. Bankruptcy is a legal and institutional decision that is driven by different circumstances in different jurisdictions. Basically, if a company is worth less than its liabilities, somebody else will always have to pick up the tab. The question is: Who? Bankruptcy is the procedure for determining who picks up the tab.

Creditor Rights and Emerging Market Debt

Abigail L. McKenna, CFA
Managing Director and Portfolio Manager
Morgan Stanley Investment Management
New York City

In order for investor participation in emerging market debt to continue its recent growth, abuses of creditor rights must be curtailed. Although bondholders have contributed to the problem by failing to exert the type of vigilance necessary to keep debtors honest, even savvy bondholders are vulnerable to abusive treatment by emerging market debtors. Ultimately, bondholders must organize in order to force such improvements as stronger covenants, greater transparency, standardization of documentation, and a better framework for resolving default crises.

The global financial system has fundamentally changed, with bond investors from diverse institutions worldwide assuming an increasingly critical role in providing capital to emerging market countries. One of the most noteworthy changes in global finance over the past decade has been the emergence of the capital markets as the major source of funding for emerging market countries. In fact, the global financial system now functions with the implicit assumption that capital markets financing for emerging markets will increase over the next few decades.

The participation of existing investors/creditors and further expansion in the global investment base depends on robust confidence in the capital markets, including the integrity of information, the good intentions of debtors, and the standing of legal contracts. Emerging market bonds, like all bonds, are contracts that define the rights of investors and the obligations of issuers. One might expect that investors entering into contracts with issuers who have a checkered history of repayment would demand significant protections. Emerging market bond investors, however, have been extremely lackadaisical when evaluating bond contracts and have only recently made a proactive effort to enhance their rights as creditors.

This presentation examines the current state of contractual rights in emerging market bonds, discusses flaws in the existing architecture of the emerging capital markets, and proposes a few changes. A case study of the default in Ecuador demonstrates some of the challenges investors face in the emerging debt markets. Finally, this presentation describes how emerging market debt investors have recently organized to counteract objectionable behavior on the part of borrowers and investment bank underwriters. I will describe the Emerging Markets Creditors Association (EMCA) and its mission to enhance creditor rights in the emerging markets.

Bond Contracts Matter

One of the dirty little secrets of the investment management industry is that portfolio managers often do not read prospectuses. And even when they do, the disparate nature of the buy side makes it difficult for any single portfolio manager or analyst to influence the terms and contractual provisions of an entire transaction. Moreover, bond covenants tend to get overlooked until something goes wrong. In the past few years, however, rising defaults in emerging markets (and in the domestic investment-grade and high-yield corporate markets) have led to greater scrutiny of the protections (or lack thereof) afforded creditors in bond contracts.

A bond is a financial instrument, but it is also a series of promises, the most important of which is the borrower's promise to repay the lender on a specified date. Associated with this promise is a sequence of covenants designed to protect the lender by setting rules that will be followed if payment problems develop. Bond covenants are also intended to provide some reassurance to investors that they will be treated fairly and will be protected from a wide range of potential abuses. But bond covenants are only as powerful as the statutory regime under which they are enforced. Without a fair judicial system in which to bring claims and a statutory framework that holds borrowers accountable for broken promises, bond covenants are worthless.

In the U.S. investment-grade corporate and high-yield markets, investors understand the benefits and limitations of the statutory regime (the Sherman Act, the securities acts of 1933 and 1934, or the Trust Indenture Act) and the resolution mechanisms (Chapter 11 or Chapter 7). Emerging market investors do not enjoy the same degree of clarity. Even though most emerging market sovereign bonds are issued under the governing law of New York or the United Kingdom, enforcement against sovereign states can be very difficult, and the resolution mechanism in the event of a sovereign default is poorly defined. The judicial system for externally issued, hard-currency emerging market debt is provided, in general, by the courts of G–7 countries. The legal framework is provided by the laws that make the use of foreign judicial systems possible: the U.S. Foreign Sovereign Immunities Act (FSIA) and the U.K. State Immunities Act (SIA). Bonds issued by emerging market sovereigns in their own domestic markets (usually denominated in the local currency of the issuer) are subject to the laws of the emerging country itself. Thus, it seems reasonable that markets assign little or no value to covenants of domestically issued emerging market sovereign bonds.

Rights of Bond Investors

Investors in emerging market sovereign debt currently benefit from a limited number of contractual rights. An emerging market sovereign bond typically contains a handful of covenants, although they are fewer in number than those found in domestic investment-grade corporate bonds or comparably rated domestic high-yield bonds. Two of the most important covenants in emerging market sovereign bonds are the sovereign issuer's agreement to waive its sovereign immunity and the issuer's agreement to submit to the jurisdiction of the United States or United Kingdom. Without these two covenants, enforcement of contractual rights would be nearly impossible, and the absence of these two covenants would render worthless most of the other covenants or protections given to the bondholders.

If a sovereign issuer defaults on debt that contains a waiver of sovereign immunity and an agreement to submit to the issuing jurisdiction, investors can bring a claim under the FSIA in a U.S. court rather than in the sovereign's court system. For example, a judgment in favor of creditors would allow for the attachment of sovereign assets in the United States. Some emerging market issuers, such as Russia, do not waive their sovereign immunity, and a few others do not agree to submit to judicial systems in foreign jurisdictions. Most sovereign issuers, however, do waive immunity and do agree to submit to the jurisdiction of U.S. or U.K. courts.

Other covenants that are typically found in emerging market sovereign bond contracts include the following:

- An event-of-default clause, which typically is triggered only upon the nonpayment of principal or interest.
- A modification and amendments clause that requires a 100 percent approval threshold to change the bond's financial terms, such as the coupon, cash flow schedule, maturity, or currency of the bond.
- A modification and amendments clause that allows a subset of bondholders (50 percent to 75 percent of the total) to change a bond issue's nonfinancial covenants, such as the waiver of sovereign immunity and the submission to jurisdiction.
- A negative pledge clause in which the borrower is typically prohibited from granting secured status to other existing unsecured creditors or future creditors.
- A pari passu clause that stipulates that the bond issue's debt service payments (interest and principal) must rank at least equally with those of existing and future bond issues.

Unfortunately, covenants have become increasingly porous over the past decade, and a few emerging market issuers have found ways to circumvent the previously mentioned covenants. This trend is true not only for emerging market bonds but also for U.S. corporate bonds, both high yield and investment grade.

An additional characteristic of the emerging bond markets is that little standardization of covenants exists among the various emerging market sovereign issuers. At the moment, issuers or underwriters have little incentive to make their bond documents more transparent, because many investors do not even read or evaluate the covenants. The burden rightly falls on the buy side to devise an acceptable standard set of covenants and to insist that better covenants be included in all future transactions. The development of basic standards and codes would make bond analysis much easier. Currently, covenants must be analyzed on a case-by-case basis, which often requires specific and expensive legal expertise.

Credit Rating Volatility

In practice, investors have demanded fewer covenants from investment-grade issuers than they have from lower-rated issuers in both the emerging and corporate markets. But to assume that ratings are going to be stable over long periods of time is simply not realistic. Historically, emerging market credit ratings have been more volatile than domestic corporate credit ratings, but the recent examples of rapid credit deterioration in the investment-grade corporate market might render the current distinction between typical high-grade and high-yield covenants passé. Although many investors have not been focused on the specific details of bond covenants when evaluating investment-grade debt, they will likely pay more attention going forward. The investors in "fallen angels" and newly distressed debt are extremely interested in the debt contract details, such as the definition of what constitutes a default, the specific wording of a negative pledge clause, or the bond's amendment and modification provisions in the event that the borrower's payment capacity is called into question. Weak covenants will decrease the likelihood that distressed investors will provide support for fallen angels. Covenants can also affect the severity of losses suffered in a default situation, because weak covenants make it easier for the debtor to circumvent negative pledge clauses, subordinate the existing debt, or coerce bond investors into less than optimal restructuring. Over the past few years, issuers have been gradually carving away at investor protections, with the tacit endorsement of investment bank underwriters and the seeming indifference of investors.

To underscore the instability of credit ratings in emerging market debt, **Figure 1** shows the Standard & Poor's ratings for Argentina, Russia, South Korea, and Uruguay from the end of 1995 through early 2002. Argentina's credit migrated south quite quickly. Russia demonstrated an interesting turnaround story, defaulting and recovering. South Korea suffered a rapid and dramatic fall from grace, dropping from AA to BB in a few months. And Uruguay, which was recently rated investment grade by at least one of the rating agencies, is now teetering on default. In retrospect, it was imprudent for investors not to insist on better protections in their bond documentation, regardless of the bond's ratings at the time of purchase.

Current Shortcomings in Default Resolution

A number of problems plague the existing framework for resolving sovereign defaults, with the chief problem being that no real framework is in place. No Chapter 11 equivalent exists for sovereign borrowers, and it is difficult to imagine one that would function well. No entity oversees the process of sorting out creditor claims, and no advocate for creditors is recognized in the restructuring process. Another complicating factor in emerging market debt restructurings is the likely involvement of at least four distinct creditor groups—foreign bondholders (mainly investors in the United States and Europe), local investors, international financial institutions (IFIs) (such as the International Monetary Fund [IMF], the World Bank, and others), and bilateral lenders (other sovereign governments). These groups often have widely divergent perspectives and motives.

The differences between creditor groups are part of the reason that contracts are so critical in emerging market debt. Foreign bondholders are de facto (although not de jure) subordinated investors. This

Figure 1. S&P Credit Ratings for Argentina, Russia, Korea, and Uruguay

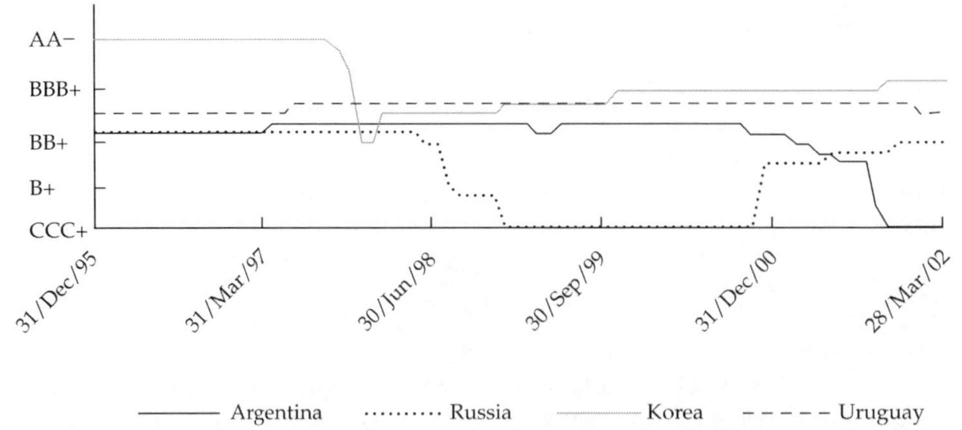

effective subordinate status should influence the way investors think about emerging market debt, particularly with regard to how they expect to be treated if the borrower cannot honor its obligations. The incentives that affect borrower behavior shift for a variety of reasons during periods of duress, and none of the incentives favors foreign bondholders; political incentives favor local investors and diplomatic incentives favor IFIs and other bilateral debtors. During a crisis, "sticking it" to "rich" foreign bankers and investors can be a politically popular move. The IFIs gain de facto senior status because their willingness to extend credit to troubled borrowers becomes particularly important during crises. Countries in crisis tend to borrow heavily from the IFIs, taking on a large debt load before they default. The IFIs usually insist that the debt owed to them is senior to all the sovereign's other bonds and loans. Bilateral lenders (i.e., other sovereign governments) often lend for noneconomic reasons but then demand comparability to other investors.

In theory, sovereign borrowers need 100 percent investor agreement on restructuring terms in order to cure the default. In actuality, however, no court system exists to oversee negotiations and to approve and enforce restructuring terms in the face of holdouts by a small number of investors. This 100 percent requirement is arguably too rigid both for debtors in real distress and for investors who want to see a fair restructuring take place. Another problem is that a single borrower may have issued bonds under a variety of jurisdictions and thus faces different and potentially conflicting requirements when attempting to restructure. In a crisis, emerging market borrowers tend to avoid a direct dialogue with their bondholders. Borrowers typically claim that bondholders are so globally dispersed that communicating with them is impossible and that the only way to effectively restructure emerging market debt is through a "take it or leave it" exchange offer. Ironically, those same debtors have no trouble finding or talking to globally dispersed investors when they want to sell them their bonds.

In the past, debtor countries in distress have engaged in a number of "rogue behaviors," such as participating in undisclosed purchases of their own debt while in default, entering into side deals with certain bondholders, exhibiting preferential treatment for certain creditors, using exit consents aggressively or abusively, and implementing stonewalling tactics aimed at preventing dialogue with bond investors. Certain creditors also employ "rogue behavior" when they buy debt at distressed levels and then try to sue sovereigns for full payment without ever intending to negotiate a restructuring. Empirically, however, more frequent abuses have been committed by debtors in default than by so-called "rogue" investors. In fact, not one restructuring has been prevented from moving ahead by the actions of holdout creditors. Moreover, creditors have been willing to act early and constructively, as evidenced by the spontaneous formation of bondholder committees in the cases of Russia, Ecuador, the Ivory Coast, and Argentina. Creditors have never delayed or prevented completion of a restructuring.

Unlike corporate bond investors, who rely on Chapter 11 or Chapter 7 to ensure the fair treatment of their claims, investors have no clear method and little precedence for how emerging market debt claims will be treated. This uncertainty is ripe for abuse, and investors cannot assume that all claims will be treated on a par (face amount or accreted) basis. In the past, some restructurings favored certain creditors, whereas others have treated all bond claims equally. Another concern relates to the fact that sovereign debtors almost always own or control significant portions of their own debt. The emerging market sovereign issuer itself may own the debt, or it may be owned by the central bank, the domestic banking system, domestic pension funds, or other local institutions. In the event of a crisis, the government can assert control over how these local investors vote on restructuring questions. Because this control can be used to affect restructuring terms, investors need greater protections from voting fraud in the restructuring process.

Investment bank underwriters of emerging market securities are unequivocally conflicted. In emerging debt markets, the same investment bank may underwrite debt, hold proprietary positions, advise sovereigns in distress how to restructure their debt, and be paid fees for this advice, as well as underwrite the restructured debt exchanges used to cure defaults. Investment banks have little incentive to represent the interests of bondholders and, in fact, are often working against bondholders in the restructuring context.

Proposed Framework for Restructurings

Three proposals have been made for dealing with the current uncertainties related to restructuring emerging market debt—one apiece from the EMCA, G–10 countries, and the IMF. Only the EMCA proposal validly addresses the concerns shared by most investors. Although the G–10 proposal tries to eliminate some aspects of uncertainty in the restructuring process, it primarily addresses uncertainties viewed as unimportant by bondholders. The IMF proposal seems to raise more concerns than it resolves.

EMCA has proposed standardizing and strengthening emerging market bond covenants. In particular, the EMCA proposal would rebalance the rights and obligations of debtors and creditors in a way that levels the playing field. The EMCA proposal includes a cram-down mechanism with an appropriately high threshold that would facilitate fairer restructurings.

The G–10 proposal includes clauses that would make restructurings easier to accomplish and would rely substantially on collective action clauses. This proposal would take legal recourse away from individual bond investors, placing it in collective hands (similar to the function of Chapter 11 bankruptcy proceedings in U.S. corporate defaults). The G–10 is actively encouraging emerging market sovereigns to include its proposed clauses in their bond contracts. But this proposal does little, if anything, to protect or enhance creditor rights.

The IMF is working on a sovereign bankruptcy mechanism that would be loosely akin to Chapter 11. Investors have many concerns about the IMF's sovereign default resolution mechanism (SDRM) proposal, but chief among them is the spurious analogy between a sovereign bankruptcy mechanism and Chapter 11 bankruptcy legislation. Whereas private companies are subject to the jurisdiction of a bankruptcy tribunal, under an SDRM, sovereign debtors would not be subject to the appropriate checks and balances that legitimize a bankruptcy regime and make it fair and effective. Investors also fear that the IMF's SDRM would appeal to the political forces in emerging markets that seek easy alternatives to policy discipline, obfuscating the need for corrective action. Additionally, because the SDRM would apply only to external bond debt, it would effectively create a subordinated class of debt. Moreover, this selective coverage would limit the SDRM's applicability to only a small number of cases because most recent crises were triggered by external debt of the private sector or domestic debt of the sovereign (as was the case with Korea and Russia).

Case Study: Ecuador

The following case study of Ecuador's default demonstrates some of the weaknesses in the existing architecture supporting the emerging debt markets. Investors who bought Ecuadorian bonds after the country defaulted did well financially, but the route that led to their recovery was dreadful. Ecuador was a catalyzing event in emerging debt markets because the coercive, almost abusive, restructuring process drove bond investors to join together to prevent similar abuses in the future.

Throughout its restructuring process, Ecuador maintained a policy of unequal treatment for different groups of creditors. Ecuador forced most of the restructuring burden on its foreign bondholders. Ecuador did not restructure its domestic debt or its debt to the IMF, the World Bank, or other IFIs. Nor did Ecuador get equal amounts of debt relief from its G–7 bilateral creditors. The Ecuadorian government refused to hold any meaningful discussions or negotiations with foreign bondholders. In fact, Ecuador avoided communication with bondholders for 12 months and then offered only a take-it-or-leave-it exchange.

Many investors believe that, during this 12-month period of silence, Ecuador engaged in a seemingly purposeful effort to drive down its bond prices in advance of the exchange offer. By the time the offer was made, the financial terms of the exchange were better than the reduced expectations prevailing in the market. Certainly, investors who bought bonds after the default at 18 cents on the dollar were willing to replace them with bonds worth 30 cents on the dollar. Nevertheless, neither those investors nor the investors who held the bonds at the time of the default were well served by the ultimate exchange offer made by Ecuador.

Ecuador's restructuring approach was coercive because of its take-it-or-leave-it approach and its threat of covenant stripping. Investors had no opportunity for basic due diligence and little time to evaluate the terms of the offer. And Ecuador chose to pursue an exchange offer rather than an amendment to the bond indenture because an amendment would have required 100 percent of investors to agree. When investors agreed to the proposed exchange, however, they also had to agree to change or eliminate some of the other covenants of the outstanding bonds. Thus, the restructuring process used "exit consents" to effect the bond exchange.

Exit consents have become popular tools in the emerging bond markets and may become more common in other bond markets as well. Exit consents can be an appropriate tool at the end of a negotiation process that has created a consensus among a super majority of existing investors, but in cases in which there are no discussions with investors and no opportunities for investors to conduct due diligence, they are coercive.

The covenants stripped out as a result of the Ecuadorian bond exchange included the cross-acceleration and cross-default clauses, a covenant that required the issuer to cancel existing bonds, and a covenant that required listing on an exchange. This last change meant that as long as a majority of the investor community agreed to the exchange, the holdouts would be left with a much less liquid and less valuable investment, not only because the remaining bond issue was smaller but because secondary market pricing and liquidity would no longer be available. Ecuador also considered using exit consents to rescind its waiver of sovereign immunity and to change the jurisdiction of the bond issue so that investors who did not participate in the exchange would no longer be able to bring legal claims in U.S. or U.K. courts.

Additional examples of the abusive use of exit consents can be found in the market for emerging market corporate debt. Some exit consents have forced investors to remove a requirement that the issuer provide financial statements in English. A Chinese company took this approach and thereafter published its reports only in Mandarin. The same company also eliminated a covenant that made the bond eligible for future debt-for-equity conversion and other kinds of benefits. Such machinations leave the bondholder with a dilemma: If the investor does not agree to the proposed exchange but enough other investors do, the security the investor is left with is tenuous.

Emerging Market Creditors Association

EMCA was founded in 2000 and has been effective in providing a singular voice for the buy side in matters concerning emerging market debt. The association was established when seven large institutional investors concluded that the rogue behavior of debtors and improper actions of investment bank underwriters would eventually make bond contracts meaningless and potentially damage confidence in the asset class. Within its first year, 40 large institutional investors joined the association.

Investors in emerging market debt founded EMCA for several reasons. Chief among them were protection of the asset class and the desire of bond investors to ensure that their interests in policy matters and market practices were represented accurately to sovereign borrowers and the official sector—the IFIs. EMCA also provides a vehicle for issuers to speak directly to bond investors and allows unbiased feedback on best market practices and on issues related to bond restructurings. EMCA also encourages information exchange among investors. Sometimes, something as simple as an e-mail to invite investors to a meeting can galvanize a critical mass and force an issuer to address its problems. EMCA also facilitates discussions about potential problems or rogue debtor behavior. For example, one member might alert others that there is something erroneous or misleading in a certain issue's documentation.

A year ago, EMCA formed a creditor rights working group to study the issue of covenants for emerging market sovereign bonds and bank loans. This move was precipitated not by any official sector initiative but by its concern about the lack of consistency and lack of standardization in emerging market sovereign bond covenants and between bond and loan contracts. EMCA recently drafted model clauses and a bond documentation checklist that emerging market investors can use for comparative purposes.

Additionally, EMCA allows investors to share resources and legal costs in matters of common interest. For example, when peculiarities were recently detected in Brazil's bond documentation, the existence of the association allowed investors to share the cost of hiring a law firm to investigate and explain the implications of the anomaly. In 2001, the association funded a legal review and comparative analysis of the key covenants of major bond issuers. Although many investors had hoped that the rating agencies might adopt this role as an added business line (i.e., ratings for covenants), nothing indicates that they intend to undertake such an effort.

Conclusion

Abuses of creditor rights in the emerging debt markets will continue unless (and until) investors organize to combat them. Confidence in the asset class will suffer in the absence of organized activity. Investors can and should join together to pressure the sell side to better represent investor interests. Collectively, bond investors will be able to counteract the aggressive or coercive behavior of issuers and underwriters. The investor community will gradually demand and receive stronger covenants, greater transparency, and standardization of documentation across various markets and issuers. By uniting (as through EMCA), the buy side can exert collective pressure on issuers and the sell side. After all, the buy-side investor is the one decision maker when it comes to investing in emerging market debt.

Enhancing Creditor Rights for Bond Investors

Christopher L. Gootkind, CFA
Vice President and Director of Fixed-Income Research
Wellington Management Company, LLP
Boston

Losses recently suffered by bondholders highlight the need for stronger creditor rights. Greater scrutiny and comprehension of the language in bond indentures are vital. To truly enhance creditor rights, however, bondholders need to join together to strengthen covenants and demand better disclosure.

Credit deterioration and volatility continue to afflict the bond market and highlight the shortcomings of credit ratings.[1] A single-point rating alone cannot adequately capture the two elements of risk: default probability (or as Moody's KMV calls it, expected default frequency) and loss severity. Beyond the limitations of the current rating systems, the lack of covenants remains a serious problem that negatively affects the security of corporate bondholders' investments.

Our very simple investment objective as investment managers in general is to give our clients back more money than they gave us. In fixed income, this objective is met by owning debt instruments for which our analysis shows the issuer will make interest payments on a timely basis and repay principal at maturity. Too often, managements take actions that are ostensibly intended to maximize returns for shareholders but are injurious to creditors (for example, leveraging up the balance sheet to make an acquisition or to buy back stock). This scenario, compounded by a difficult credit environment in which many heavily indebted companies have stumbled badly, underscores the need to focus on creditor rights in order to help achieve clients' objectives.

This presentation will highlight the importance of creditor rights. After explaining the reasons for focusing on creditor rights and describing what these rights are, I will outline the priority of claims in a voluntary Chapter 11 bankruptcy to explain where bondholders stand and what they can expect in terms of repayment. I will then explore three case studies—AK Steel Corporation, Rite Aid Corporation, and Owens Illinois—that hold important lessons for bondholders in terms of the need for stricter bond covenants. Last, I will discuss the purpose of creditor committees and will present an industry action plan for improving creditor rights. Even though I am not an expert in bankruptcy or debt restructuring, I believe that bondholders should be proactive and work together to enhance and enforce our rights as creditors.

Why Focus on Creditor Rights?

Given the losses bondholders have suffered in the past year, the need for stronger creditor rights is obvious. Bondholders have recently been exposed to the following fraudulent business practices (and their perpetrators):

- undisclosed off-balance-sheet liabilities (Enron Corporation),
- undisclosed rating triggers (independent power producers),
- undisclosed—or poorly disclosed—bank covenants (NRG Energy),
- fraud (WorldCom and Adelphia Communications Corporation), and
- management malfeasance and dubious accounting (Tyco International and Qwest Communications International).

[1]This presentation builds on my presentation at the 2001 AIMR fixed-income conference. See "Improving Credit Risk Analysis," *Fixed-Income Management for the 21st Century* (Charlottesville, VA: AIMR, 2002).

In some cases, these practices resulted in bankruptcies. Other cases resulted in major credit rating downgrades that led to precipitous declines in bond prices, and further downgrades may yet occur.

Regardless of the fraud cases, another reason to worry about creditor rights is the sheer number of large bankruptcies that have occurred recently. **Table 1** lists the 10 largest companies that filed for bankruptcy in the United States since 1980 and the amount of each company's assets at the time of filing. Seven of these ten largest bankruptcies occurred in 2001 and 2002. WorldCom, which had more than $100 billion in assets before it declared bankruptcy, was the largest bankruptcy in U.S. history. WorldCom financed about $30 billion in assets with long-term debt, representing at least $24 billion in bonds widely held by investors.

The number of defaults has also risen. **Figure 1** shows that the ratio of credit downgrades to upgrades, measured by both the number of issuers and the dollar amount of affected debt, has increased to a level that is equal to or higher than the level in the early 1990s, which was the last bad credit environment. The dollar amount has become enormous because of recent large, high-profile defaults. The default rate for the trailing 12 months as of August 2002 is currently about 10 percent, and Moody's Investors Service is predicting a 2003 default rate higher than 8 percent. Given that most investors consider 2 percent to be the typical default rate in the high-yield sector, these numbers are extremely high. Loss severity has also increased. Historically, when a bond defaulted, its price fell to 45 or 50 cents on the dollar, but recently, some defaulted bond prices have plunged to 10 or even 2 cents on the dollar.

Table 1. Ten Largest U.S. Companies to File for Bankruptcy since 1980

Company	Bankruptcy Date	Total Assets Prebankruptcy
WorldCom	21/Jul/02	$103,914,000,000
Enron Corp.	2/Dec/02	63,392,000,000
Texaco	12/Apr/87	35,892,000,000
Financial Corp. of America	9/Sep/88	33,864,000,000
Global Crossing	28/Jan/02	25,511,000,000
Adelphia Communications Corp.	25/Jun/02	24,409,662,000
Pacific Gas and Electric Co.	6/Apr/01	21,470,000,000
MCorp	31/Mar/89	20,228,000,000
Kmart Corp.	22/Jan/02	17,007,000,000
NTL	8/May/02	16,834,200,000

Source: Based on data from www.bankruptcydata.com.

Figure 1. Speculative-Rated Downgrade-to-Upgrade Ratio, 1987–June 2002

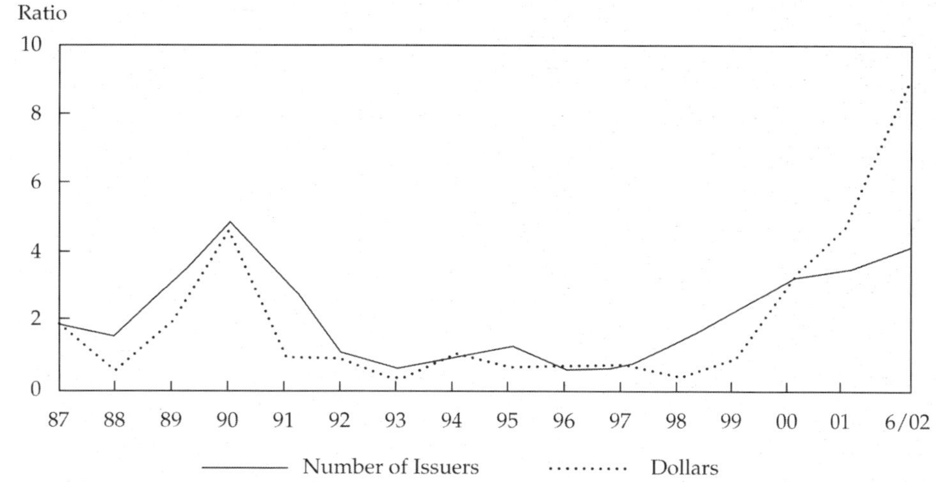

Source: Based on data from Moody's Investors Service.

The number and dollar amount of downgrades has also become a problem. **Figure 2** shows the dollar amount of debt affected as a result of "fallen angels" (bonds that have been downgraded from investment grade to high yield) compared with the dollar amount of bonds that qualify as "rising stars" (bonds that are upgraded from high yield to investment grade). Fallen angels have forced many fixed-income managers to sell because of client guidelines that require holdings to be investment grade. In the high-yield market, fallen angels have become huge percentages of managers' benchmarks, as discussed by Stephen Kealhofer.[2] When WorldCom was downgraded to below investment grade, it still had $15 billion in market value of publicly held debt ($30 billion par at 50 cents on the dollar), which represented a substantial 3.5 percent of the high-yield market.

When managing versus a benchmark, a manager who wants to be neutral on an issuer in terms of credit exposure versus the benchmark needs to hold the same percentage of an issuer as is in the index. A manager can minimize tracking-error risk by owning benchmark weights of the issuers that have higher amounts of debt outstanding (i.e., that represent the larger positions in the index benchmark). But it seems counterintuitive to me that the more debt an issuer has, the more a portfolio manager should feel he or she has to own the debt of that issuer simply because it constitutes a large portion of a benchmark. The more highly indebted an issuer becomes, the riskier it is. For example, investing 3.5 percent of a portfolio in a troubled issuer, as would have been the case for WorldCom, is a highly risky bet. In the late 1990s, Japan accounted for about 22 percent of the Salomon World Government Bond Index (WGBI), but most investors would agree that having such a large percentage of a portfolio invested in any single issuer is imprudent. High yield now faces a similar concern. Some of the fallen angels, such as WorldCom and Qwest, have such large amounts of debt outstanding that investors must be wary of how closely their managers mirror the benchmark.

Benchmark weighting is not the only problem with fallen angels. Most companies rated investment grade have bank lines that are unsecured. Their loan covenants are relatively loose, consistent with relatively loose bond covenants. When companies are downgraded to high yield, however, banks become more concerned about being repaid. As a result, when a bank line comes due after a company has been downgraded to high yield, banks typically demand collateral as security before rolling over the loans, which structurally subordinates bondholders. So, investment managers face further subordination on top of weak bond covenants. In addition, when companies are downgraded to high yield, they lose access to short-term funding in the commercial paper market. And because investors have become more concerned about lending to riskier companies, the commercial paper market for BBB rated (A2 or lower short-term rating) issues has shrunk dramatically.

[2]See Mr. Kealhofer's presentation in this proceedings.

Figure 2. Dollar Amount of Affected Debt for Fallen Angels versus Rising Stars, 1995–August 2002

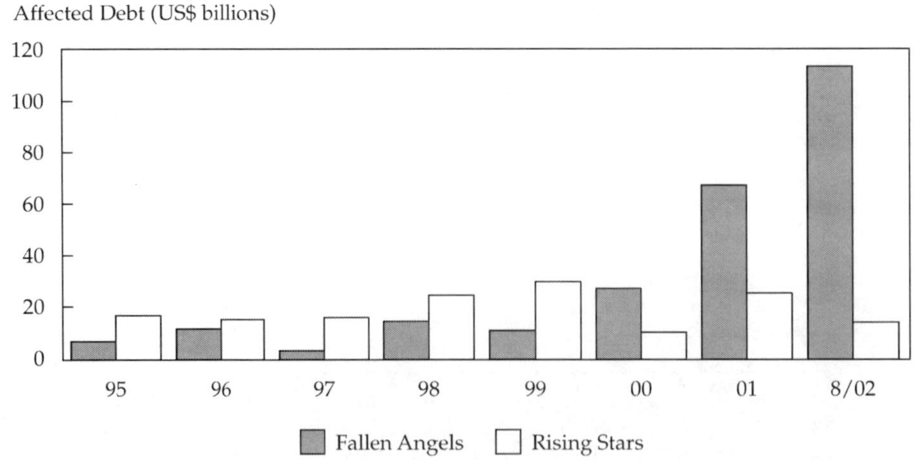

Note: Fallen angels = issuers downgraded to high yield from investment grade; rising stars = issuers upgraded from high yield to investment grade.

Source: Based on data from J.P. Morgan Chase & Company.

What Are Creditor Rights?

Creditor rights are spelled out in the indenture—the contract between the bond issuer and the bondholder—which specifies, for example, the time period for repayment, the amount of interest to be paid, whether the bond is convertible into equity of the issuing company (and if so, at what price or ratio), and the amount of principal that is to be repaid.

The indenture's provisions outline what the borrower can, cannot, and must do. The provisions are meant to protect bondholders. Indenture provisions might include the following:

- a limit on the amount of total indebtedness,
- filing financial statements on a timely basis,
- a full audit once a year,
- the maintenance of a positive net worth, and
- a negative pledge clause.

Bondholders should always keep in mind that a company's management and board of directors are beholden to shareholders—first and foremost. In fact, under normal operating conditions (i.e., the company is solvent), management has a fiduciary duty to shareholders and no corresponding obligation to bondholders or creditors, except to abide by the language of the controlling bond indenture. When lending money to a company, therefore, bondholders must carefully review the indenture and its provisions. Consider the case of Marriott Corporation when it split into two companies in 1993. The court ruling determined, to the detriment of bondholders, that as long as no specific provision of the bond indenture was being violated, management had a fiduciary responsibility only to shareholders.

Priority of Claims

Only when a company is insolvent does management's fiduciary duty shift to creditors, and even then, bondholders do not have first claim on a company's assets or pledged collateral. Understanding the priority of claims in a bankruptcy is critical. In a voluntary Chapter 11 filing, the bondholder ranking in the capital structure vis-à-vis other claimants can have a huge effect on what the bond's ultimate recovery value will be.

At the top of the capital structure is debtor-in-possession financing. After (or immediately before) a company files for Chapter 11, it often has to borrow from banks to get funding as it reorganizes its finances and operations. These lending banks, which provide the debtor-in-possession financing, get a superpriority lien above and beyond other creditors in order to allow the company to continue to operate until it exits Chapter 11. Secured creditors are next in line. These creditors typically include working capital lenders, the government (if property or similar taxes are owed), and lessors that might have security, such as aircraft-leasing companies or real estate lessors. Any first mortgage debt also appears at this level of priority. Administrative and other priority claims come after secured creditors. These claims include wages, tax claims (unrelated to property), professional fees (e.g., fees for bankruptcy lawyers and financial advisors), and any trade creditors who have to be paid to keep the business running.

Only after administrative and priority claims have been paid are general unsecured creditors allowed to stake their claim. General unsecured creditors include vendors, the U.S. Internal Revenue Service (for back income taxes), and bondholders. Bondholder claims are prioritized according to their ranking in the capital structure. Senior unsecured debt ranks higher than subordinated debt. Off-balance-sheet claims, whether from leases or litigation, follow, and shareholders are last. A preferred stock investor has a senior claim over a common stock shareholder, but shareholders are often wiped out when a company files for Chapter 11.

Even though management has an obligation to act in creditors' best interests during bankruptcy proceedings, a problem arises in that secured creditors' interests are not always aligned with those of unsecured creditors. In effect, everyone is fighting over the leftovers, a situation that creates an uneasy dynamic. Furthermore, management may resent working for creditors. Management's personal interests are not necessarily aligned with their new fiduciary responsibilities. For example, management's stake in the company may likely be wiped out in a reorganization, with claims paid to satisfy the creditors.

Case Studies

The following case studies demonstrate why bondholders need to know and understand the details of an indenture and why they need to fight for stronger indenture provisions.

AK Steel. AK Steel is an example of a "consent solicitation." One of the bond issues of AK Steel included a restricted payments basket that limited the company's ability to pay preferred dividends. However, because of distressed conditions in the steel industry and covenant restrictions, AK Steel stopped paying dividends in the fourth quarter of 2001 (which covered three quarters). According to the terms of the preferred stock, if the company did not pay preferred dividends for six consecutive quarters, preferred stockholders (which included unionized employees) could name two additional directors to the board. Not wanting to add two new union-influenced board seats, AK Steel's management asked bondholders to modify the restricted payments basket in the indenture in order to enable the company to pay preferred stock dividends. To entice bondholders of that issue to agree to the modification, AK Steel offered a quarter-point consent payment ($2.50 a bond) to the bondholders who agreed. The majority of bondholders did consent, thus slightly weakening the indenture protection by letting more cash flow out of the company. Shortly thereafter, the preferred stock was redeemed.

Usually, only a simple majority is required to amend indenture language, so large bondholders can sometimes collaborate to effect a particular course of action. In this case, the trade-off for bondholders was reasonable because, although they lost some debt protection in the form of cash flow being paid out to preferred stockholders, they were paid a fee to compensate for the loss. If bondholders are unhappy with the proposed consent fee, they can join together in an effort to negotiate a higher fee.

Consent solicitations can be somewhat coercive. Often, investors are driven to vote "yes" because a "no" vote means giving up the consent fee. Before consenting to an indenture modification, investors should carefully weigh the pros and cons of the change (and any fee or other compensatory benefit offered).

Rite Aid. Rite Aid, a pharmacy retailer, grew rapidly through acquisitions until late 1999, when the company disclosed several accounting irregularities. For retailers such as Rite Aid, maintaining sufficient inventory is essential and vendors are vital to that process. When Rite Aid's vendors stopped extending credit to the company after the accounting irregularities were announced, Rite Aid turned to banks for the liquidity needed to keep its shelves stocked. But once the banks realized the extent of Rite Aid's accounting problems, they refused to lend to the company without being granted collateral as security. Rite Aid had no choice but to succumb to the banks' demands. To get a $1 billion secured loan facility, Rite Aid had to have its subsidiaries guarantee the facility and pledge their assets as security.

At the time, Rite Aid bondholders thought they were in good shape because the bond indenture contained a negative pledge clause. Negative pledge means that if the bondholders do not have security, no other creditors get security, but if other creditors get security, then bondholders must receive the same security. In this case, Rite Aid received a new secured loan, but the bondholders did not get secured status. How did this happen?

The fine print from Rite Aid's unsecured note indenture (Section 10:10) reveals how Rite Aid circumvented the pledge: "The company covenants and agrees it will not, and will not permit any Restricted Subsidiary to create, issue, incur, assume, or guarantee any Secured Debt without making effective provision . . . (for the bondholders)." Secured debt was defined as "indebtedness for money borrowed, which is secured by a mortgage, pledge, lien, security interest on property of the company, or any Restricted Subsidiary." A Restricted Subsidiary was defined as "any subsidiary, whether existing on or before the date of this indenture, unless such subsidiary is an Unrestricted Subsidiary." An Unrestricted Subsidiary was defined as "any Subsidiary, which . . . has been designated by a Board Resolution as an Unrestricted Subsidiary. . . ." In other words, a subsidiary was restricted unless the board passed a resolution that declared it to be unrestricted. Thus, the board simply passed a resolution redefining all restricted subsidiaries as unrestricted. Once these subsidiaries were deemed unrestricted, Rite Aid could pledge them as security to the banks. The banks got security, and the bondholders were left structurally subordinated.

This example serves as a warning of the limitations of negative pledge clauses. Bondholders must scrutinize the indenture definitions and interpret legalese that is designed by corporate lawyers to give the company flexibility. Bondholders are at a disadvantage because they do not have access to the same (inside) information that management has, and when covenants are being structured on a new bond issue, bondholders are fragmented and unable to present a united front in securing the desired covenants. Further, when companies begin to falter, banks obviously want to get ahead of bondholders in terms of security claims.

Of course, if Rite Aid did not possess enough assets to pledge to the banks, the company might have filed for bankruptcy and the outcome for bondholders could have been worse. Rite Aid's bonds currently trade at about 65 cents on the dollar, and the company has issued some new equity. Whether the company will succeed is yet to be seen. The main point is that bondholders do not always have the protection they think they have with a negative pledge clause.

Owens Illinois. Owens Illinois is a rare example of bondholders enhancing their position *after* a negative pledge clause was circumvented. Owens Illinois had some fundamental business problems during 2000 and 2001, but asbestos litigation against the company was the main problem. The banks, in anticipation of the company's bank credit facility coming due, were worried about Owens Illinois's asbestos liability. Before agreeing to roll over the bank debt, the banks wanted to get ahead of the asbestos claims and arranged to get a first-priority lien on a new $4.5 billion credit facility in the third quarter of 2000. The bondholders believed they were protected against such an event because the bond indenture contained a negative pledge clause. Nonetheless, in this case, the bondholders received no security despite the negative pledge, even though the banks did.

In some ways, the Owens Illinois example portrays a worse situation for bondholders than that in the Rite Aid example. With Owens Illinois, the negative pledge applied to the indebtedness of the company and required that notes (bond debt) be directly secured equally and ratably with any other debt that received secured status. Close scrutiny would have revealed the loophole—the negative pledge applied *only* to the indebtedness of the company itself and clearly cautioned that substantially all of the operations of the company were conducted through the company's subsidiaries. Owens Illinois could avoid the restrictions by changing the obligors on the bank credit facility and by pushing all bank debt to the subsidiary level.

In other words, bondholders lent money to the holding company, which also had bank debt at the time. But the negative pledge in the bond indenture applied only to the holding company, not to the subsidiaries. Because the company's subsidiaries were not included in the language of the negative pledge, the banks were able to lend new money to the subsidiaries, with the subsidiaries pledging their own assets as collateral. By using this money to pay off the bank debt at the holding-company level, the company violated the spirit, but not the letter, of the indenture because no bank debt had been secured at the holding-company level. Thus, the company's transactions did not violate the negative pledge clause.

In this case, and perhaps because of the earlier Rite Aid experience, bondholders got smart. Large bondholders joined together, hired a financial advisor, and began to negotiate with the company. The bondholders proposed a second lien, because they too wanted to get ahead of the asbestos claims. Owens Illinois agreed to this proposal because the company knew it would need bond investors to provide future financing for maturing debt. Owens Illinois launched a consent solicitation seeking to provide a second lien to all bondholders, and the bondholders agreed because their position was enhanced by the lien. Later, a new bond issue, which gave a first lien to the bondholders, was used to pay off the bank debt. To enhance their subordinated position, Owens Illinois bondholders, working together, were able to partially remedy an unfavorable situation by getting a second lien.

Again, the lesson is to read the fine print of the indenture. A negative pledge clause must contain language that includes a company's subsidiaries; the Owens Illinois covenant excluded subsidiaries. In some instances, a negative pledge clause can give an issuer flexibility by carving out a certain amount of assets that can be pledged to secure debt without requiring that bondholders also get security. The ultimate issue is the claim of the bondholders compared with the claims of the company's other lenders. In the Owens Illinois case, the banks exploited a loophole in the indenture, but bondholders were able to enhance their position because the interests of the company and its lenders were aligned; all lenders wanted to get ahead of the asbestos claims. And because Owens Illinois needed access to both bank loans and bond markets, the company was willing to provide all lenders with what they were requesting. The cost to Owens Illinois of maintaining the access it needed to the capital markets was minimal.

Covenant Wish List

The following covenants should be present in every bond indenture in order to protect the interests of bondholders. If bondholders cannot act to protect their interests in difficult markets and economic environments, such as the conditions they have recently experienced, their ability to ever do so is doubtful. Certainly, such action could never be accomplished in a bull market.

Strong Negative Pledge. The pledge should state unequivocally that if other lenders obtain some type of security or other special treatment, then bondholders must receive the same deal. Bondholders should also understand all details of the negative pledge, including possible partial carve-outs.

Springing Liens. Springing liens automatically add security to the bondholder's claim under certain circumstances. If banks have springing liens in their loan agreements and bondholders do not have the same protection in their indentures, the outcome can be highly detrimental to the bondholders. Motorola, which is experiencing financial difficulties, is an example of a company whose bank lines (but not its bond debt) contain springing liens. If the company is downgraded to BBB or BBB–, the banks will get security but the bondholders will not. So, if Motorola was downgraded by the rating agencies, the effect would likely be a multinotch rating downgrade for the bondholders. The company's bonds would probably go straight to a high-yield rating, because the rating agencies would focus on the fact that the banks' springing lien would make the bondholders structurally subordinated to the banks.

Debt Test. A debt test protects bondholders by mandating a maximum level of debt relative to the issuer's total assets and is an objective test to ensure that this level is not exceeded.

Minimum Net Worth. A minimum-net-worth covenant mitigates concerns about leveraged buyout (LBO) risk or leveraged restructurings. This type of protection is especially important in the current market environment. Both nominal and real interest rates are incredibly low, stock prices have plunged, and the spread between corporates and Treasuries is unusually wide. Thus, companies may be inclined to buy back equity, perform a leveraged recapitalization, or even execute an LBO. Consider the example of Dole Food Company. In April 2002, the company issued investment-grade bonds with virtually no covenants at 245 bps over comparable-maturity Treasuries in a low interest rate environment. In early September 2002, management announced plans to use this low-rate debt to help finance its own LBO. The lack of adequate protection, particularly the lack of a minimum-net-worth covenant, allowed Dole to undercut the position of bondholders in the seniority of their claim on the company's assets. Insisting on a minimum-net-worth covenant can protect bondholders against other companies choosing a path similar to that of Dole.

Change-of-Control Put. A change-of-control put means that if a company is acquired, the bondholders can put their bonds back to the issuer at par or at a slight premium. A change-of-control put, in lieu of a minimum-net-worth covenant, would have helped Dole's bondholders. The reality is, however, that change-of-control puts frequently exist in the high-yield market but not in the investment-grade market, where they would often be of greater value.

Asset Sale Limitations. An asset-sale-limitation covenant stipulates how the issuer must use the proceeds from a large asset sale. Bondholders prefer that if assets are sold, then the proceeds should be used to pay off not only bank debt but also outstanding bonds. For example, Qwest recently sold its high-cash-flow directory business and will use the proceeds of this sale to pay off its bank debt, not its bond debt. Which assets will remain for bondholders and what the value of those assets will be in the case of bankruptcy is an open question.

No Rating Triggers in Bank Lines. Rating triggers in bank lines of credit are detrimental to bondholders. In the past few years, an increasing number of bank lines have included such triggers, thus putting rating agencies in an awkward position. The problem came to the fore with Enron in the fall of 2001. If a rating agency downgrades a company, the result can be a self-fulfilling prophecy, because the downgrade causes the bank line to become due, or at least raises financing costs. This reaction may cause a liquidity crisis, because neither the banks nor the capital markets may be willing to roll over the debt, thereby creating a downward spiral. The rating agencies do not want to be in the business of "causing" bankruptcies, but rating triggers in bank lines often lead to this result. The fallout for bondholders is serious.

Off-Balance-Sheet Debt Limitations. There should be limitations on an issuer's amount—and type—of off-balance sheet debt, and such debt should be clearly disclosed. Special purpose entities can be especially dangerous and are subject to abuses.

Disclosure of Terms in All Other Financings. Companies are not currently required to file the terms of their bank facilities with the U.S. SEC, but investors should pressure the SEC to add this requirement. Bank loans can be publicly traded, but not knowing what sort of covenants these bank facilities might contain makes it difficult to understand the level of risk in a company's balance sheet. The terms of any and all financing must be disclosed.

Coupon Step-Up. A coupon step-up is triggered when a company is downgraded. A one-step rating change typically translates into an increase of about 25 bps in coupon; the greater the downgrade, the larger the coupon increase. (Note that coupons can step down for upgrades as well.) Coupon step-ups offer more reward for higher risk, but the lure of a higher coupon may put the bondholder in the strange position of hoping that the company gets downgraded, even if a downgrade may conflict with client guidelines.

Creditor Committees

Both informal and formal creditor committees exist. Informal creditor committees are composed of large investors who are willing to strategize and act together in the hope of benefiting from strength in numbers. The bondholders at Owens Illinois are an example of how a simple majority was able to effect some indenture modifications. Forming such a committee facilitates the process of sharing information, brainstorming, and responding to a consent solicitation. The primary drawback is that this type of creditor committee does not have any legal standing. In addition, sharing information has its pros and cons. Disclosing ownership of a sizable position in a poorly performing bond may make selling that position more difficult.

Formal creditor committees are typically established when a company is in bankruptcy, and such committees must abide by rules and regulations governing how they are formed and how they act. A formal committee has the power to influence the outcome of a bankruptcy. Membership on a committee offers an excellent opportunity to learn about negotiating strategy (which could be helpful, given that more defaults are likely in the current market environment).

But serving on a formal creditor committee also has several potential drawbacks. Restrictions prevent investors who serve on creditor committees from transacting in the bonds of the subject issuer. This restriction can present problems. For example, a manager serving on a creditor committee probably will have clients with different goals, which results in conflicts regarding whether to hold (to see if the situation improves) or to sell (to completely eliminate exposure to the situation) the subject issuer's bonds. Also, all of a manager's clients—not only the bond clients—must be treated fairly, but participation on a company's creditor committee could restrict an entire investment firm from trading any of the company's securities, including its equity. Such a restriction could disadvantage equity clients. Another consideration is the hefty time commitment required for creditor committee participation. Committee participation could also require the financial commitment of hiring a financial advisor for assistance, although these fees could typically be billed to the bankruptcy estate.

Action Plan

Reading the fine print in an indenture and identifying loopholes are the first steps in securing creditor rights. Unfortunately, new bond issues often come to the marketplace quickly, making it difficult to scrutinize and understand the provisions in the indentures. Reading the registration statements that must be filed with the SEC online at the Electronic Data Gathering, Analysis and Retrieval system (EDGAR) at www.sec.gov can be helpful, particularly if attention is paid to specific definitions, such as "restricted subsidiaries and the company" versus "the company and its subsidiaries."

Further, bond investors have to learn from past market events and personal experiences. If history is ignored, mistakes are bound to be repeated. To succeed in getting stronger covenants from issuers and investment bankers, bondholders need to collaborate. Strong covenants are an essential investor protection and, in this environment of deteriorating credit and volatile markets, are becoming ever more important. Bondholders should demand better disclosure (e.g., filing of all bank and other financing agreements). If necessary, bondholders should also demand a priority lien, as they did in the Owens Illinois example. Finally, talking to other creditors, other lenders, is crucial for securing the strongest bond covenants possible and protecting bondholders' interests.

Question and Answer Session

Christopher L. Gootkind, CFA

Question: The Rite Aid example suggests that credit analysts failed to do their job. Should the industry hire people devoted exclusively to analyzing the legal language in covenants?

Gootkind: It is crucial to have knowledgeable people review the covenant language, probably at the company level instead of the investment management industry level. The analysts don't have to be lawyers and could be investment people. It would be helpful, however, to have the investment people "trained" by attorneys in the ways covenants are drafted, how companies can circumvent them (as I've shown in this presentation), and the most effective types of covenants.

Ideally, the buy-side community should create a model indenture, which incorporates the most useful covenants and provides the protection bondholders seek. In many ways, the issue of creditor rights is more of a concern for investment-grade bond investors than high-yield investors because high-yield investors know and accept the risks of investing in a higher-risk market.

Question: Do you have any suggestions for buyers who must balance the demands of reading the indenture with the short time period available for making a decision to buy a new issue?

Gootkind: Most of the deals that come quickly to market are issued off a shelf registration, so I suggest taking the time to read the shelf registration and any other financial documents filed with the SEC before the new issue is announced (when investors are pressed for time to decide whether or not to buy the new deal). In many cases, investors can do keyword searches on databases, such as EDGAR, to look in the shelf registration database for such terms as "negative pledge," "restricted subsidiaries," or "change of control."

Question: To what extent is a bond trustee liable if it fails to monitor a company's lack of adherence to the indenture agreement?

Gootkind: The bond trustee does not have much liability. This lack of monitoring is a problem. Bond trustees need to be held more accountable for their negligence, but I'm not sure how to effect such a change. Ultimately, we need to keep company management—and the investment bankers—honest and, in the event of a breach in the indenture agreement, use substantive remedies, such as interest penalties, debt acceleration clauses, or lien granting.

Question: Do you believe leveraged bank debt has a better risk–return trade-off than straight corporate bonds because the bank debt has better covenants?

Gootkind: To clarify, leveraged bank debt is typically secured, whereas investment-grade bank debt is typically unsecured. As with unsecured corporate bonds, the covenants for investment-grade bank debt aren't that strong.

Given that distinction, certainly in this negative credit environment and likely over the long term, bank debt does have a better risk–return trade-off than unsecured corporate bonds. Should the market and the credit environment turn around, however, I believe straight, unsecured corporate debt will likely rally more than bank debt on a relative basis.

Question: Should managers allocate to bank debt to improve portfolio risk?

Gootkind: Over a long cycle, bank debt will probably outperform on a risk-adjusted basis; that is, it will likely have higher Sharpe and information ratios than will corporate bonds. This potential scenario argues for allocating some of a portfolio to bank debt.

With bank debt investing, however, two caveats are in order: First, a decision has to be made about whether you want to trade only on publicly disclosed information or have access to nonpublic information. The latter could force your firm to operate on a restricted basis from time to time or set up a barrier (e.g., a "Chinese" wall) to limit and control the flow of information. If you rely only on public information, you could be at a slight disadvantage vis-à-vis bank debt investors, who have access to nonpublic information. Second, you could have client guideline or operational (e.g., trade settlement, back-office) issues to overcome.

Question: Have you had any conversations with other investors regarding an investment-grade bondholders association?

Gootkind: Yes, but the discussions have been informal at best. Several of us think it's a good idea, but to date, no one has been willing or able to put in the time to lead the charge.

Question: Does having the sell-side firms establish and run the benchmarks perpetuate "creditor rights" problems?

Gootkind: I don't see a linkage between sell-side firms creating and managing benchmarks and problems with bondholder rights. I would say, however, that underwriters, although sympathetic to bondholders having inadequate covenants, are not likely to be at the forefront of proposing enhancements. Debt issuers are rather happy with the status quo, and sell-side firms don't want to risk jeopardizing their relationships with those clients.

Question: You and Kealhofer say that indexes are defective benchmarks, but Meyer says that indexes outperform fixed-income managers.[1] As a buyer of fixed-income management, what should I conclude?

Gootkind: Indexes may outperform fixed-income managers, at least in some environments, but indexes don't represent the "real world" in at least four important ways: First, they don't incur transaction costs (which have been very high in the rather illiquid OTC corporate and high-yield markets). Second, index rules regarding when companies enter and exit an index because of an upgrade (or downgrade) may not coincide with portfolio guidelines. For example, certain indexes use a Moody's rating to determine whether an issuer is investment grade or high yield and others use an S&P rating, or the lower of the two. Another example is that for some indexes, a downgraded issuer stays in the index until the month-end after the downgrade. A portfolio's guidelines may differ from those index rules and may require that an issue be immediately sold. Third, indexes have several thousand holdings; it's virtually impossible to replicate the index. And finally, because of the asymmetry of corporate bond returns—much greater downside risk than upside potential—very large index weightings in a given issuer shouldn't necessarily drive an investor to hold a big position in the issuer simply to match the benchmark. In the extreme, if one corporate issuer represented 20 percent of a credit benchmark, it wouldn't be prudent to put 20 percent, or any percentage close to 20 percent, in a client's portfolio. The best approach to the composition decision is to focus instead on the client's investment objectives—such as income, capital preservation, and so forth—and work to achieve a highly diversified portfolio.

[1]See the respective presentations of Mr. Kealhofer and Mr. Meyer in this proceedings.

Managing Core-Plus Portfolios

Scott E. Grannis
Director and Chief Economist
Western Asset Management Company
Pasadena, California

Investors began to adopt core-plus management several years ago because of its return potential, which was a departure from the traditional view of fixed income as a source of stability. Recent conditions (weak nominal U.S. economic growth, low yields and high credit spreads, a convexity panic, and a weak stock market) have increased the difficulty of managing core-plus portfolios and cast doubt on future investor demand for core-plus management. Critical issues for core-plus managers to consider for the future are benchmark evolution, investment guidelines, credit exposure, mortgage convexity, Treasury inflation-indexed securities, and critical core-plus components.

At Western Asset Management Company, we have accepted the challenge of managing core-plus portfolios, that is, the challenge of delivering better returns than those of a typical core or passive fixed-income portfolio without taking on excessive risk. In business school, I was taught that such outperformance was impossible to achieve, but for 13 years, I have been dedicated to doing the impossible. In fact, several fixed-income managers, such as Western Asset, PIMCO, and BlackRock, have met this challenge fairly consistently. Whether core-plus management will continue to be successful or even desirable, however, is an open question. My presentation will focus on the major issues currently facing managers practicing this investment style.

The Future of Core-Plus

Clients are thinking about their portfolios in new ways. They are asking questions they never asked before, and they are thinking about fixed income as they never have before. Just a few years ago, when fixed-income returns were 7 or 8 percent and stock market returns were even higher, investors adopted core-plus for its return potential and forgot about fixed income's role as a source of security and safety in asset allocation. Now, they are beginning to wonder whether they should return to taking their risk in equities rather than fixed income. The answer to that question is not immediately clear, but I suspect that more and more investors will want to manage their portfolios by looking in the rearview mirror; in other words, they will again view fixed income as a source of stability, not excess returns. As a result, fixed-income managers may see less interest in core-plus management in the next few years.

The goal of using core-plus portfolios is to beat the benchmark without taking on excessive additional risk, which means that managers have to balance myriad factors. At Western Asset, we manage portfolios the old-fashioned way. We do not use quantitative analysis in the construction of our portfolios, but we do in their performance and risk analysis. First, we make a duration decision and decide how to allocate that duration across the yield curve. We then choose the sectors we think will outperform and then, within those sectors, choose the issuers we think will outperform. We try to make sure that the extra risk we take on in one area is balanced whenever possible by natural hedges in another; that is, we try to add securities that have a low correlation with the new risk. In addition, given the recent upheavals in the market, we devote our attention to aspects of fixed-income management that are likely to have a large impact on core-plus portfolios, namely, benchmark evolution, investment guidelines, credit exposure, mortgage convexity, Treasury inflation-indexed securities (also known as TIPS), and the critical core-plus components—nondollar, high-yield, and emerging market bonds.

Evolution of the Benchmark

The Lehman Brothers U.S. Aggregate Index has been the benchmark of choice for most bond portfolios. **Table 1** shows how the composition of the Lehman Aggregate has evolved from 1985 to August 2002 and highlights three major shifts. In 1985, Treasuries composed 49 percent of the Lehman Aggregate Index (the largest percentage of the market that Treasuries have ever reached), but by August 2002, that share had declined to 22 percent. Second, representation of mortgage-backed securities (MBS) has doubled; MBS now make up more than one-third of the index and have become a larger component of all fixed-income portfolios as a result. Finally, the credit (corporate) sector grew from 19 percent of the index in 1985 to 26 percent by August 2002. Clearly, these changes to the benchmark have been huge, and because managers must pay attention to the benchmark, their management style has also been changed to reflect the changes in the composition of the fixed-income market during the same period.

Table 1. Lehman Aggregate's Composition

Asset Type	August 2002 ($7.6 trillion)	1985 ($1.7 trillion)
Agency	13%	10%
Credit	26	19
Mortgage backed	36	18
Other	4	4
Treasury	22	49

The quality distribution within the credit sector of the Lehman Aggregate has also changed. Between 1973 (when Lehman Brothers first started keeping the statistics) and August 2002, the index has experienced a significant increase in all of the lower-quality sectors of the bond market, as indicated in **Table 2**. The BBB sector has risen to 35 percent from 9 percent, while the AAA sector has fallen to 10 percent from 27 percent. These changes mean that anyone who uses the Lehman Aggregate as a benchmark has recently become exposed to much more credit risk than ever before. To make matters worse, at the same time that investors were beginning to realize that BBB corporates had become a larger portion of their portfolios, Enron Corporation, WorldCom, and other such corporate disasters struck. Needless to say, many investors, who often did not realize the extent of their credit risk exposure, lost a lot of money. A number of Western Asset's competitors who took outsized risks have suffered serious repercussions. Not surprisingly, the clients of these firms may be wondering why they chose the Lehman Aggregate as a benchmark.

Table 2. Quality Deterioration of Lehman Aggregate's Credit Sector

Rating	August 2002	1973
AAA	10%	27%
AA	19	31
A	36	33
BBB	35	9

This situation has been exacerbated by the steady migration to core-plus management in the past decade. In 1993, core-plus represented about one-third of "core" (i.e., assets benchmarked to broad market benchmarks, such as the Lehman Aggregate) fixed-income assets under management with Western Asset, but by 2002, core-plus assignments accounted for about two-thirds of "core" assets under management. Core-plus has gained broad acceptance among plan sponsors and other investors over the past decade, but I predict that core-plus growth will stop dead in its tracks for a while. I do not know whether the number of core-plus managers will shrink, but I doubt that many investors will be adding new core-plus mandates. In addition, despite the historically attractive characteristics of core-plus, the credit shocks in the market that have occurred over the past year may trigger reconsideration of existing core-plus mandates.

Investment Guidelines

Adhering to investment guidelines is always critical, but it is especially important in managing core-plus portfolios. At Western Asset, we manage money for many pension funds, most of them defined-benefit plans, but at least half of our client base consists of other account types, including foundations, endowments, corporate cash, and so on. Venturing beyond the core fixed income sectors requires great care. Typical investment guidelines for core portfolios restrict the manager to investment-grade bonds and to the Lehman Aggregate as the benchmark, which is composed of investment-grade bonds with a maturity of one year or more. In addition, clients may also give the manager the flexibility to hold up to 10 percent in below-investment-grade bonds and may authorize the use of futures and options, primarily in the context of risk management. Core-plus portfolios allow a larger allocation away from the benchmark and a broader range of assets.

Table 3 shows the typical breakdown of assets within our core and core-plus investment guidelines compared with the benchmark (the Lehman Aggregate). In core portfolios, we currently underweight the Treasury sector and overweight the credit and mortgage sectors. As noted earlier, the credit sector

Table 3. Typical Investment Guidelines

Asset Type	Benchmark[a]	Core	Core-Plus
Agency	13%	4%	1%
Asset backed	3	2	4
Credit	26	33	30
Emerging market	0	na	5
Mortgage backed	36	44	41
TIPS	0	7	6
Treasury	22	10	2
High yield	0	na	5
Non-U.S.	0	na	6

na = not applicable.

[a]Lehman Aggregate, as of August 2002.

Figure 1. Corporate Credit Spreads, 31 January–31 August 2002

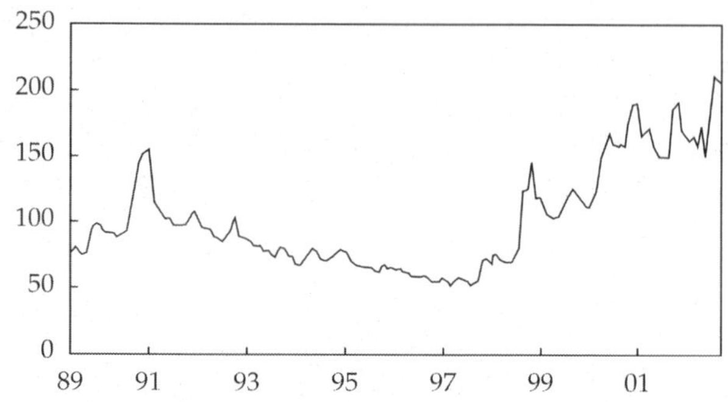

Source: Based on data from Lehman Brothers.

may include some non-investment-grade bonds. A core-plus mandate typically allows us to use non-dollar, high-yield, and emerging market bonds. We invest in these three sectors at our peril because they are not included in the benchmark and are often not highly correlated with it. As Table 3 indicates, we are accommodating these added sectors by reducing the allocation to the credit and mortgage sectors relative to the respective allocations of core portfolios.

Credit Exposure

Because the amount of credit exposure in many fixed-income portfolios has risen substantially, managers should carefully analyze the risk–reward trade-offs when making decisions about duration, yield curve, and sector weightings.

Credit spread is a measure of the reward for owning corporate bonds—the higher the spread, the greater the potential reward. But high spreads are also indicative of a great amount of perceived credit risk. As **Figure 1** illustrates, credit spreads have been increasing for five years and have never been higher since Lehman began collecting data in 1973. The 1997–02 period has been the worst bear market for corporate bonds since the 1930s. Corporate spreads have increased in successive waves: The first wave occurred in 1998, with the Russian and Long-Term Capital Management crises. In 1999, another increase in spreads was Y2K related, when investors were seeking to reduce their risk exposure in general (i.e., in anticipation of potential technological failures at the beginning of 2000). In 2000, another big increase in spreads occurred when the Fed tightened in an attempt to slow the economy.

The end of 2000 appeared to be a propitious time for core-plus managers to overweight corporate bonds, but as soon as they did, spreads increased yet again as the economy plunged into recession. And in the first half of 2002, just when it seemed the recession had ended, the WorldCom debacle pushed spreads even wider. At Western Asset, we believe a good case can now be made for beginning to overweight corporates because we think they finally offer adequate compensation for the risk of owning them, given the context of an economy that is growing, albeit at a moderate pace, inflation that is low, and a Federal Reserve that is willing to be accommodative.

Duration Mismatch

Today, many investors who use their fixed-income portfolios to hedge a liability stream find themselves with a duration mismatch between their assets and their liabilities. Investors, particularly defined-benefit pension plans, buy fixed-income securities as a hedge for their fixed-pay liabilities. In recent years, the Lehman Aggregate, the benchmark of choice for most bond assets, has had a duration of 4–5 years, whereas the duration of the liabilities of most defined-benefit plans has been 10, 15, 20, and even 25 years. By accepting this duration mismatch, plan sponsors were implicitly betting that interest rates would not fall. But as interest rates hit a generational low this year, this duration mismatch began to work against plan sponsors, and at the same time, their equity holdings were devastated. Many plan sponsors are now realizing they have a desperate need to invest in longer-duration investments to minimize this mismatch risk.

For this reason, a number of our core-plus clients have recently indicated an interest in switching to a longer-duration mandate. In the mid-1990s, when 30-year yields were at 7 and 8 percent, we could not persuade clients to implement long-duration mandates. We would suggest that they increase the duration on their bond assets to match the duration of their liabilities, but no one was interested. Ironically, now that yields have fallen by half, clients have become more interested in long-duration assignments—not because they are truly comfortable with long-duration assets, but because they have reached the conclusion that they cannot accept the risk of this asset/liability mismatch any longer. Plan sponsors have lost too much of their surplus, and their funded ratio has dropped severely; they are being forced to cut their risk, that is, their exposure to underfunding their liabilities. So, just as some fixed-income investors are pulling out of the long-term bond market because they think interest rates have bottomed, other investors, particularly pension plans, are marching in.

Relative Yields. Figure 2 depicts yields on the government and nongovernment sectors of the Lehman Aggregate, along with the ratio of these yields. Yields in both sectors are at 40-year lows, and the relative spread between the two (the ratio of the two) is at a 40-year high. Shifting from the government to the nongovernment sector can increase yield by 60 percent. In nominal terms, this spread may not seem significant, but in relative terms, it is. In this brave new world of extremely low yields, an increment of 100 bps over a yield of 4 percent is quite considerable.

Yield Curve. Figure 3 shows the shift in the Treasury yield curve from May 2000, when yields were at their peak, to September 2002. Normally, in a falling interest rate environment, investors would instinctively follow a strategy of buying the longest-duration bond in anticipation of the highest relative return. From a risk–reward perspective, however, the part of the yield curve to invest in is the one in which yields are expected to decline the most.

Figure 2. Lehman Aggregate: Government versus Nongovernment Yields, 27 February 1976–31 August 2002

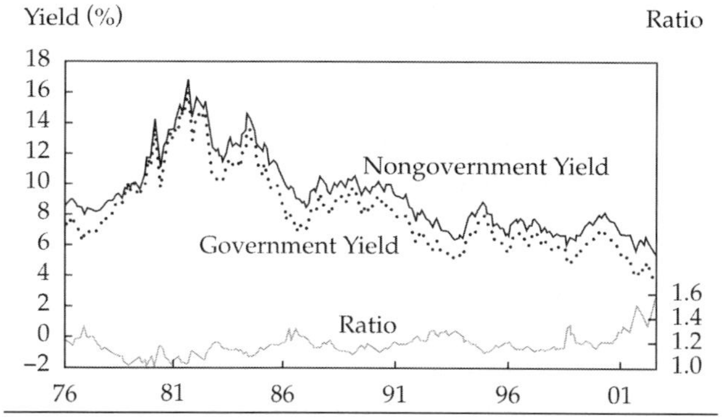

Source: Based on data from the Lehman Brothers Aggregate Bond Index.

Figure 3. Treasury Yield-Curve Shift, 8 May 2000–11 September 2002

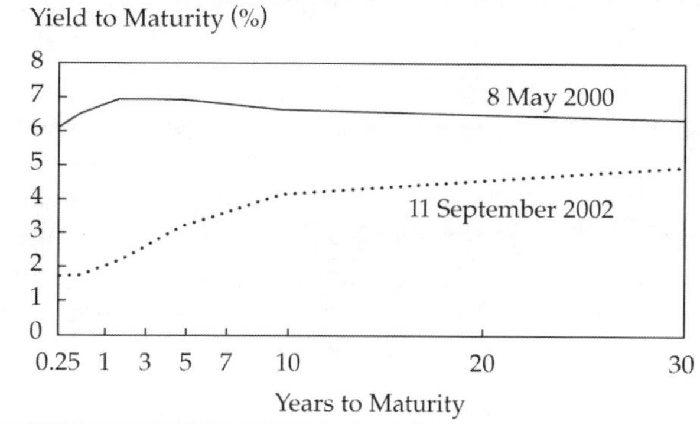

Source: Based on data from Bloomberg.

An investor who believed in May 2000 that the Federal Reserve was going to cut short-term rates from 6 percent to less than 2 percent would also have guessed that the curve would steepen, as it did. This situation presents a quandary to the investor: With falling rates, a longer-duration bond would—at least on the surface—appear to be the most desirable investment, but if short-term rates fall relatively more than long-term rates, investment in the short end of the yield curve may, in fact, yield better results. To increase value in a falling interest rate environment relative to a benchmark with a duration of roughly five years, a portfolio needs a longer duration than the benchmark, say, six or seven years. Yet to capture the benefit of the steepening curve, the portfolio also needs to overweight short-term bonds, a strategy that is difficult to implement.

Managers cannot perform such a feat unless they have the ability to use futures and options. Typically, the way to make such a play on the yield curve has been to buy Eurodollar futures or Eurodollar call options, moves that set off alarm bells at the custodian bank and with consultants. Suppose, for example, that a manager wants to add a year of duration to a typical $100 million fixed-income portfolio in order to lengthen duration relative to the benchmark, but only wants to add duration at the front end of the yield curve. If the manager uses Eurodollar contracts, each with a notional value of $1 million and a duration of one-quarter of a year, the manager has to go long about $400 million of notional value, or 4,000 contracts. Some investors and consultants would claim that the portfolio would now be leveraged 5 to 1 (because of the exposure to the $400 million Eurodollar contracts in addition to the $100 million long bond position in the portfolio), when the actual effect is to lengthen the duration of the portfolio by only one year, which is not very much. A further implication of this example is that leverage in a fixed-income context is meaningless; the only true measure of risk is duration. We always try to convince our clients (especially for core-plus assignments that give us full investment discretion) not to worry about leverage. Our goal is to make sure we are managing duration according to the client's mandate and within reasonable limits. We have been fighting this battle with clients and consultants for more than 10 years.

Market Expectations. Market expectations of Federal Reserve policy determine the steepness of the yield curve. **Figure 4** shows historical three-month LIBOR, market expectations of future three-month LIBOR as of 26 November 2001, and market expectations of future three-month LIBOR as of 31 August 2002. Because LIBOR and the federal funds rate are closely linked, the expectations for LIBOR are driven by anticipated Fed behavior. At the end of 2001, the market indicated that the economy was headed for a V-shaped recovery. The yield curve became very steep because of the belief that a series of future Fed-tightening moves would raise short-term rates; the federal funds rate was expected to climb to almost 4 percent by the end of 2002. As often happens, the market was wrong. The expected Fed tightening did not materialize and is now forecast to occur in mid-2003. Accordingly, the front end of the yield curve has been relatively flat.

Although short rates are driven by market expectations of Fed actions, inflation drives long-term bond yields. **Figure 5** suggests that with inflation hovering around 1 percent, long bond yields could fall further.

Figure 4. Actual versus Expected LIBOR, 1 January 2000–31 December 2005

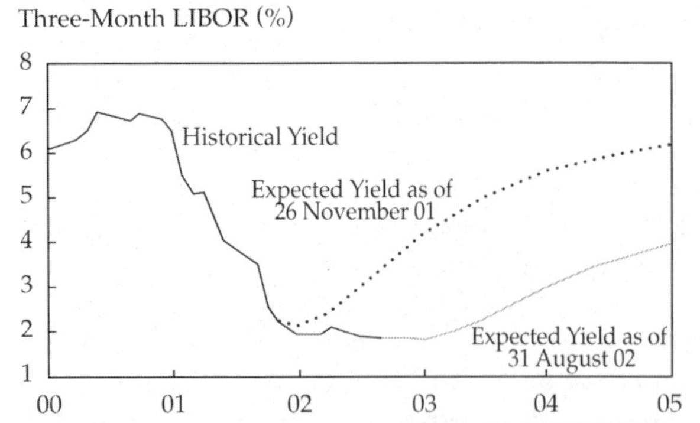

Source: Based on data from Bloomberg.

Figure 5. Inflation versus Bond Yields, 31 January 1971–31 August 2002

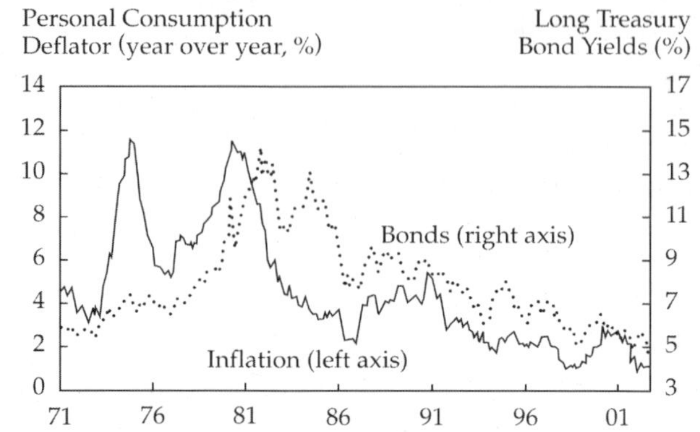

Source: Based on data from the Bureau of Economic Analysis, the Federal Reserve, and Bloomberg.

Mortgages

Freddie Mac and Fannie Mae are desperately trying to find the right asset/liability duration match in their portfolios. The convexity of the mortgage market, which has never been as vicious and volatile as it has been in the past few months, is a huge problem. With such tremendous swings in the duration of mortgages, some investors may be getting seriously hurt, and the volatility and losses we are seeing now may be merely the tip of the iceberg.

Mortgages have suddenly become securities with extremely short durations. **Figure 6** compares 10-year Treasury yields, which have typically been the benchmark for the mortgage sector, with the duration of the MBS sector in the Lehman Aggregate. In most periods, the duration of mortgages has been three or four years. But when Treasury yields fall, mortgage duration also falls as homeowners prepay their mortgages more rapidly. Recently, the duration of the mortgage sector fell to 0.75 years. (Note that this occurred too recently to be reflected in Figure 6.) Mortgage durations have never been so short, and Treasury yields have never been so low. Approximately 90 percent of the mortgages in the United States are eligible for refinancing, and borrowers have been able to refinance at ever lower rates.

The result has been a "convexity panic," or a scramble for duration, as managers who are overweight MBS relative to the benchmark watch their portfolio duration shorten relative to the benchmark. If managers do not want their portfolio duration to shorten as a result of falling interest rates (when longer duration is desirable), they have to replace duration lost in the MBS sector with 10-year Treasuries or other long-duration securities. A vicious cycle

Figure 6. 10-Year Treasury Yields versus MBS Sector Duration, 31 January 1991–31 August 2002

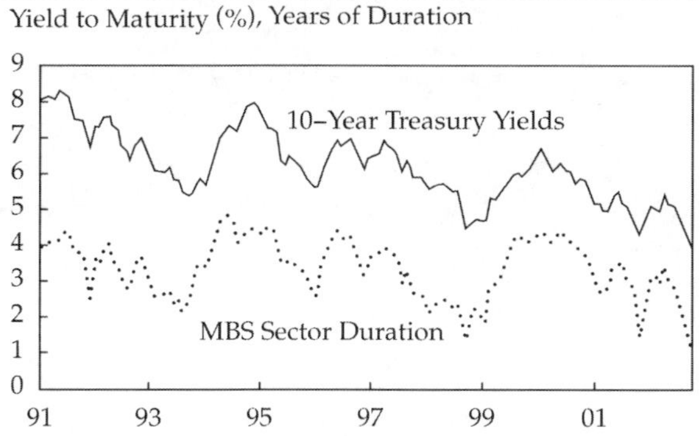

Source: Based on data from Bloomberg and Lehman Brothers.

Figure 7. Real Yields versus GDP, 31 March 1997–30 June 2002

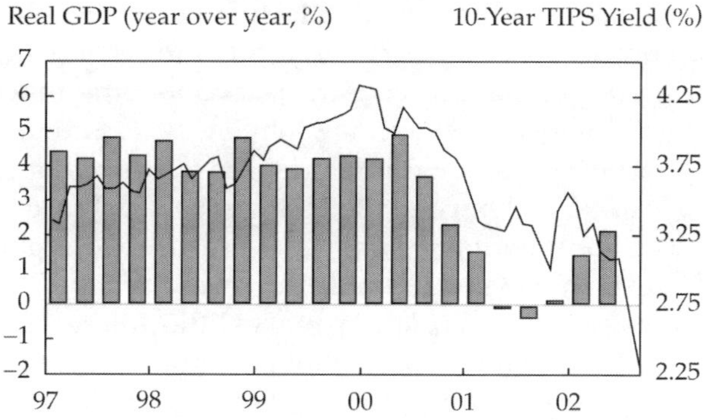

Source: Based on data from Bloomberg and the Bureau of Economic Analysis.

ensues. Rising demand for Treasuries causes yields to fall even further, leading to rising mortgage prepayments and even shorter mortgage durations. Instead of owning a bond, MBS investors now effectively own cash.

As a consequence, a serious cost accompanies a large exposure to MBS. Because their duration is so volatile and because they have become such a large portion of the benchmark, MBS affect all duration decisions. Managers have to be able to manage the duration of their portfolios as the duration of MBS changes, a feat that requires hedging, a lot of guesswork, and the use of futures and options. Hedging MBS can be costly, especially in a volatile market. Think of investing in MBS as the equivalent of owning a Treasury and selling a call option on it. In effect, an MBS investor is betting on low volatility by selling someone else protection from falling yields in exchange for some expected extra yield. In normal times, the MBS investor can keep this premium, but in volatile times, this portfolio protection becomes very costly. Right now, Freddie Mac, Fannie Mae, and investment managers could be losing a great deal of money, a situation that needs to be carefully monitored.

TIPS

We currently include TIPS—the top-performing financial asset class for the past four years—in our core and core-plus portfolios. Recent market action, however, is making us question their future role. TIPS has been one of the most interesting nonbenchmark sectors and have been the best-performing asset when real yields are falling. Their real yield is now about 2 percent, as shown in **Figure 7**. A 30-year TIPS has a duration of about 18.5 years, whereas a 30-year Treasury has a duration of only 13 or 14 years.

Many managers have incorporated TIPS in portfolios as an inflation hedge, because their nominal yield is equal to their real yield plus realized inflation (as measured by changes in the U.S. Consumer Price Index). We, too, include TIPS in our portfolios for their inflation-hedging abilities but also as a hedge against a weak or deflationary economy. Even though a lower inflation rate will decrease TIPS returns, the Fed typically lowers the real federal funds rate if the economy slows and inflation falls. This action tends to result in lower real yields on TIPS, causing TIPS to perform well because of price appreciation.

Our research indicates that the expectation of Fed easing has driven the TIPS market for the past several years, or at least it did until two months ago. The significant drop in TIPS' yields in recent months, as shown in Figure 7, has not been accompanied by any change in market expectations of Fed policy. Rather, the TIPS market has been driven primarily by the decline in 10- and 30-year Treasury yields. Whereas TIPS used to be driven by the short end of the curve, they are now being driven by the long end of the curve. They no longer work as a hedge against recession or deflation because, in a sense, they are already priced for a recession. TIPS are now more of a substitute for long Treasuries than they are a hedge against a weak economy. We think their value now lies in being a more attractive investment than Treasuries.

Core-Plus Assets

Managers can add nondollar, high-yield, and emerging market bonds to a core portfolio to create core-plus portfolios.

Nondollar Bonds. Not long ago, a manager who bought Italian bonds and played the convergence of Italian yields to sovereign yields in the rest of Europe could have made a fortune. Since the introduction of the euro, however, most of the economies of the industrialized countries have become much more closely linked and few obvious excess return opportunities among industrialized country bonds have appeared beyond the U.S. market. At Western Asset, the nondollar bonds we use in a core-plus context are sovereign debt, primarily in the G–15 countries. Country selection makes little difference in the current context, but nondollar bonds can provide a significant diversification benefit. Even though the correlation between nondollar and U.S. bonds has increased and their yields are about the same, nondollar bonds are not perfectly correlated with U.S. bonds, and thus, managers can invest in nondollar bonds to reduce the overall risk of a portfolio without sacrificing any yield. Indeed, managers can even pick up a bit of yield these days by investing in nondollar bonds.

An additional opportunity in the nondollar area lies in placing yield-curve bets. **Figure 8** depicts market expectations for various central bank rates. As of August 2002, the market was not expecting any rate changes: The Fed was expected to keep its rate at 1.75 percent; the European Central Bank, around 3 percent; and the Bank of England, about 4 percent. Is the 200 bps differential between the Fed and Bank of England rates justified? The pound sterling has long been solid against the dollar and inflation has not been a problem in England, so we think the Bank of England's repo rate is likely to fall and to converge with the federal funds rate. If such a convergence between major central bank rates occurs, managers can use global yield curves to find potential undervalued situations.

The problem with nondollar bonds is currency risk. Changes in exchange rates can swamp the returns on bonds if currency exposure is left unhedged. At Western Asset, we have decided that currency risk and fixed-income portfolios do not mix. Incorporating all the data available for the 17 years ending 31 March 2002, **Figure 9** depicts the risk–reward potential of hedged and unhedged non-U.S. government bond indexes, the Lehman Aggregate, and a U.S. government index. The returns among the indexes differ little, but the risk of an unhedged portfolio is far greater than that of a hedged portfolio. We recommend that our clients use a hedged benchmark but that we be provided with a modest degree of latitude to leave currency exposure unhedged if we see a significant return opportunity in doing so.

Figure 8. Expected Short-Term Rates: Bank of England, European Central Bank, and U.S. Federal Reserve, 1 January 1999–31 August 2002

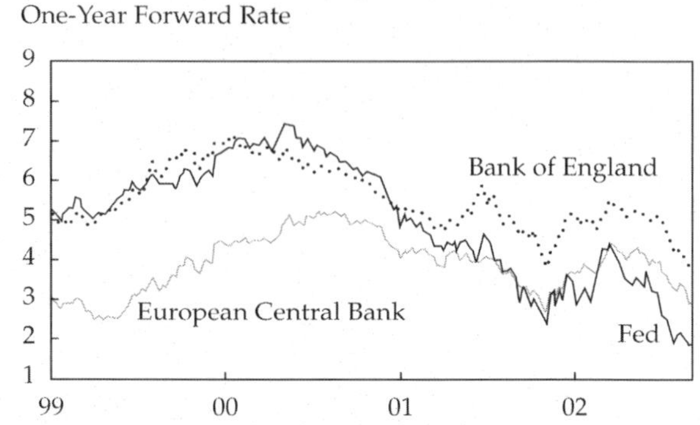

Source: Based on data from the London International Financial Futures Exchange and Chicago Mercantile Exchange: 4th LIBOR contract less 25 bps.

Figure 9. Risk–Reward Trade-Off of Hedged versus Unhedged Non-U.S. Bonds, 31 March 1985–31 March 2002

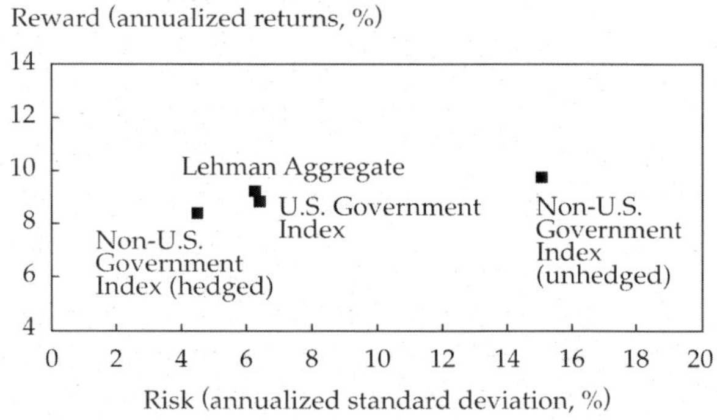

Source: Based on data from Lehman Brothers and Salomon Brothers.

High-Yield Bonds. High-yield bond spreads to Treasuries have been volatile and have recently reached record highs, as shown in **Figure 10**. Spreads this high imply that the market thinks an investor who purchases a diversified portfolio of high-yield bonds with maturities of about 10 years will see half of the issuers in the portfolio enter bankruptcy over the lives of the bonds. This assumption is fairly dramatic, however, and we think the probability of such massive default rates is significantly lower than what the market is forecasting. Spreads have remained high simply because the market is extremely wary of corporate bonds after all the bad news of recent years, leaving value on the table for the astute investor to pick up.

Figure 10. High-Yield Spreads versus Treasuries, 1 January 1997–31 August 2002

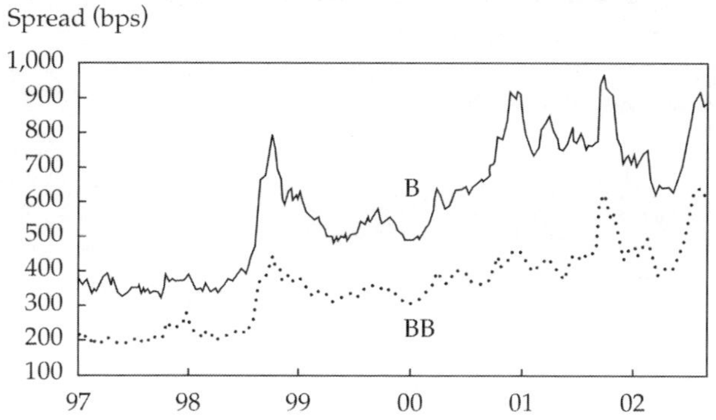

Source: Based on data from Chase Securities.

Managers have two choices with high-yield bonds. They can buy several high-yield bonds (credits) that they like, or if they are worried about defaults but think the sector is attractive, they can buy small positions in many different issuers, as we are doing at Western Asset. We currently devote about 5 percent of our core-plus portfolios to the high-yield sector, and our exposure is extremely diversified, as shown in **Table 4**. We are essentially betting that the sector will improve but do not want to make any issue-specific bets; that is, we want to minimize our event risk.

Emerging Market Bonds. Emerging market spreads have also been extremely volatile, as shown in **Figure 11**. As is the case with high-yield bonds, these spreads, currently about 700 bps over the Lehman Aggregate, imply that about one-half or more of sovereign borrowers backing these issues will default in the next 10 years, which we think is an extreme assumption. This sector, although sometimes treacherous, can be advantageous as long as exposure is limited. We currently maintain our emerging market exposure at 5 percent in a core-plus portfolio and invest in seven countries, as shown in **Table 5**. We buy only liquid sovereign issues. We think that managers who buy a diverse selection of bonds in the emerging market universe and hold them for 10 years can be expected to outperform the Lehman Aggregate.

Table 4. Typical High-Yield Exposure

Sector	Allocation
Basic industry	9%
Capital goods	11
Consumer noncyclical	16
Energy	7
Finance	11
Gaming	9
Homebuilders	3
Lodging	2
Media cable	4
Media noncallable	9
Other consumer cyclical	2
Retail	1
Technology	1
Transportation	3
Utility	9
Wireless	1
Wirelines	1

Figure 11. Emerging Market Spread ex Argentina, 31 January 1994–31 August 2002

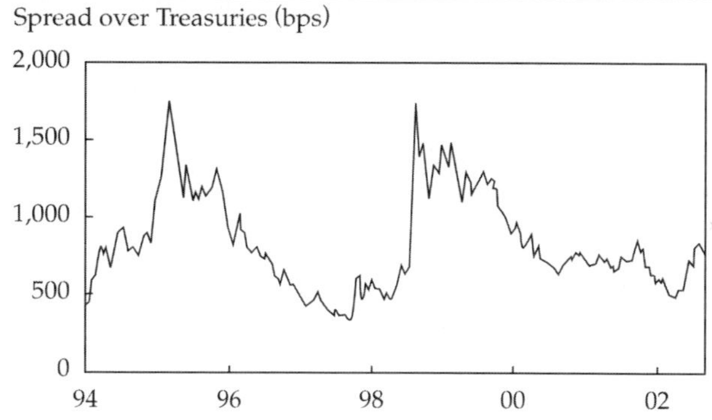

Source: Based on data from the J.P. Morgan Emerging Markets Bond Index.

Table 5. Typical Emerging Market Exposure

Country	Allocation
Brazil	35%
Bulgaria	16
Colombia	8
Panama	10
Peru	10
Philippines	13
Russia	8

Conclusion

These are interesting times, not simply because of such corporate debacles as Enron and WorldCom or the deflationary situation in Japan, but because of the sheer number of nasty, awful, nerve-racking events that are occurring. In the United States, we are experiencing the weakest nominal growth recovery and the lowest rate of inflation in decades; yields, particularly in the Lehman Brothers U.S. Aggregate universe, are the lowest and credit spreads are the highest that they have been in our lifetime; a full-fledged "convexity panic" is under way, with Freddie Mac and Fannie Mae at its center; and the stock market is the weakest it has been since the Great Depression. Such factors have increased the difficulty of meeting the basic challenge of managing core-plus portfolios. Whether core-plus managers will continue to do the impossible—and whether clients will still want us to try—remains to be seen.

Question and Answer Session

Scott E. Grannis

Question: What is the appropriate defensive posture for a core-plus portfolio, and have core-plus managers been as successful in being defensive as they were in being aggressive during the bull market?

Grannis: Managing core-plus portfolios is more of an art than a science. The mandate of a core-plus assignment is to outperform the benchmark portfolio, which entails taking on extra risk. A manager who runs a core-plus portfolio defensively will probably not be able to fulfill the core-plus mandate for reasons that I hope I made clear in my presentation. A core-plus manager has to be willing to balance risks and to seek natural hedges. For example, TIPS can be a hedge to a long-duration exposure, although this is not true at the present time.

Question: Do you use total-return swaps to control security-level risk in high-yield or other sectors?

Grannis: We use total-return swaps, but in the investment-grade rather than the high-yield sector. Three years ago, we hardly knew what swaps were, but now we are asking clients to authorize their use and approximately one-third of our clients have done so. The buy side of the fixed-income market became interested in swaps when the U.S. Treasury was running surpluses and many thought Treasuries would disappear. Even though we are again faced with deficits, I think swaps will continue to become more important in managing portfolios. A manager might decide, for example, that she likes some corporate names but is nervous about the economy. Instead of selling the corporates and buying them back later, a swap enables her to buy protection against a general widening in spreads.

Question: How many issues do you hold in a typical core-plus portfolio, and do you impose any limit on issuer concentration?

Grannis: Approximately one-third of a typical core-plus portfolio is in investment-grade corporates, with about 80 different issuers. We aim to be diversified, so our average exposure to any one issuer is less than 0.5 percent of the total portfolio. We impose a concentration limit of about 1.5 percent per issue, but only a handful are held at levels greater than 1 percent. The majority of issues range from 0.25 to 0.75 percent of the portfolio. In this particular market, observing such limitations has been one of the keys to survival. If a manager were to hold a 3 percent position in a few issuers, each of which turned out to be the next WorldCom, the manager could be out of business. We confronted such problems in the early 1990s and learned our lesson then.

Question: What is your opinion of using the Lehman Brothers Global Aggregate Index as a benchmark for core-plus portfolios?

Grannis: About 10 years ago, investors began to be interested in global bonds, but that lasted only a couple of years because not many people knew how to manage them well. Subsequently, we have noticed more interest in using global bonds opportunistically as in a core-plus mandate. Nonetheless, investors in the United States have slowly adjusted to adding non-dollar bonds to their portfolios and seem to have decided that they should give managers the whole range of fixed-income sectors to use as a toolbox. So, interest in global mandates has resurfaced, but not by leaps and bounds. Although we recently haven't seen a great deal of interest in global bond portfolios, I think the Lehman Global Aggregate would be the best choice as a benchmark, and indeed, it is the one that we are recommending.

Investing in Emerging Market Debt

Mohamed A. El-Erian
Managing Director
Pacific Investment Management Company
Newport Beach, California

Emerging market debt has consistently outperformed emerging market equities, and this trend is likely to continue. Although the emerging market debt asset class has a positive secular trend, the cyclical outlook is challenging. In approaching this asset class, investors who focus on the fundamentals should be able to identify enough quality credits to obtain significant return and downside protection.

Emerging market debt is an inefficient asset class and is often in the news because of negative events. But it is also an asset class that has produced some good performance results over a number of years. However, despite being an attractive, albeit imperfect, asset class, emerging market debt has struggled to establish itself in investors' asset allocation processes. This lack of acceptance stems from a number of factors: information failures, technical imbalances of the asset class, relative valuation issues, and historical volatility.

Three factors have influenced the development of this asset class. First, its complexity and volatility are the result of having been on the receiving end of a highly fluid global environment. It is also affected by a number of initiatives, as described by Abigail McKenna,[1] that are intended to reform the global financial architecture. Second, the major credit crises that have occurred in the past several years—Argentina's default in 2001, Russia's in 1998, and others—have raised investor concerns about international contagion (i.e., the extent to which one country's economic troubles can contaminate another country's financial markets).[2] These negative perceptions of "credit events" have slowed the development of a dedicated investor base, despite solid returns, good diversification potential, and improving volatility characteristics. Third, the asset class has gradually matured in terms of creditworthiness, information accuracy and availability, market infrastructure, and investor base.

Looking ahead, the expected continuation of the factors just described suggests a high volatility short-term outlook characterized primarily by a difficult external environment and political risk, particularly in Brazil and Turkey but also in other countries. The long-term outlook is better. The desire to invest in these markets is strong and is supported by the improving creditworthiness of the asset class.

This presentation is divided into three parts. First, I will discuss the basic characteristics of the asset class—the good, the bad, and the ugly. Next, I will describe Pacific Investment Management Company's (PIMCO's) investment process for the asset class. Finally, I will discuss current market conditions and future prospects.

Characteristics of the Asset Class

The multiyear performance record of emerging market debt is good, as shown in **Table 1**. The J.P. Morgan Emerging Markets Bond Index Plus (EMBI+) outperformed the other major bond indexes for the past seven years, despite the Russian default in 1998 and the biggest sovereign default in history by Argentina in 2001.

Indeed, since 1990, emerging market debt has outperformed a variety of other major asset classes, such as the Lehman Brothers Aggregate (LBAG), Lehman Brothers High Yield (LBHY), S&P 500, and MSCI EM Free, as shown in **Figure 1**. Interestingly, the 16 largest emerging markets' global debt funds managed to navigate through the Argentine default

[1] Please see Ms. McKenna's presentation in this proceedings.
[2] For further information on this topic, see Roberto Rigobon, *International Financial Contagion: Theory and Evidence in Evolution* (Charlottesville, VA: Research Foundation of AIMR, 2002).

Table 1. Past Annualized Return of Various Asset Classes for Various Periods Ending 30 June 2002

Period	Salomon World Government Bond Index	Salomon Broad Investment-Grade Index	Lehman Credit-Grade Index	Lehman BBB Index	Lehman International BB Index	EMBI+
1-Year	13.96%	8.51%	7.50%	5.18%	–0.83%	–5.19%
3-Year	4.45	8.05	7.53	6.31	3.91	9.65
5-Year	4.36	7.55	7.13	6.36	4.74	5.06
7-Year	3.71	7.26	7.08	6.68	6.41	12.49

Source: Based on data from Bloomberg Financial Markets.

Figure 1. Multiyear Returns for Various Asset Classes, 31 December 1990–31 December 2001
(value of US$1,000 initial investment)

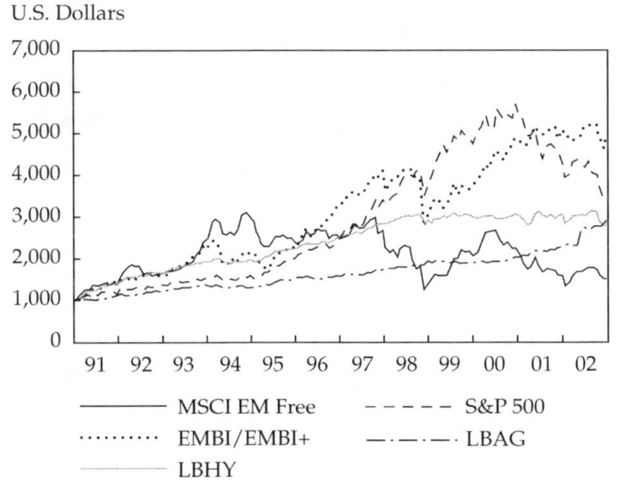

Source: Based on data from Lehman Brothers, Bloomberg Financial Markets, and Morgan Stanley Dean Witter.

Figure 2. Returns for 16 Largest Emerging Markets' Global Debt Funds, 2001
(one-year return by volatility)

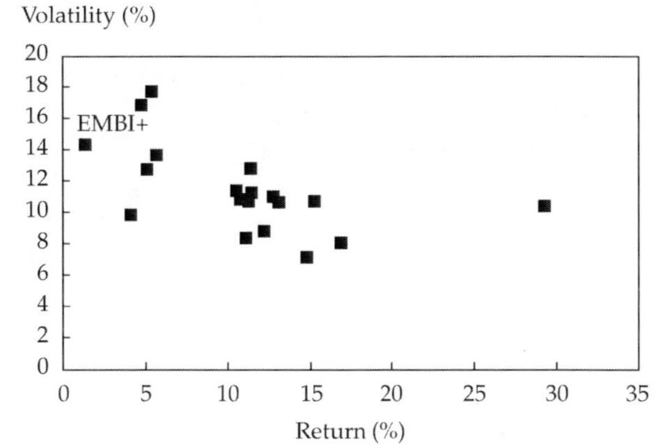

Note: Historical data as of 17 December 2001.

Source: Based on data from Merrill Lynch.

crisis in 2001, outperforming the EMBI+ by a considerable margin, as shown in **Figure 2**. This suggests that managers are learning how to deal better with these global "credit events."

Investors tend to think of emerging market debt as being more of an equity play than a bond play. The numbers, however, tell a different story. As shown in **Figure 3**, emerging market bonds consistently have outperformed emerging market equities and have gained a lot of ground during the past two to two-and-a-half years. This performance is explained by the nature of the asset class. For the most part, investing in emerging market bonds requires assuming exposure vis-à-vis sovereign or government debt. Investing in emerging market equities, however, requires taking corporate credit exposure. Under most economic conditions, a basic asymmetry exists between the risks of governments and the risks of corporations.

Figure 3. Relative Performance of MSCI Emerging Markets Equity Index versus EMBI+

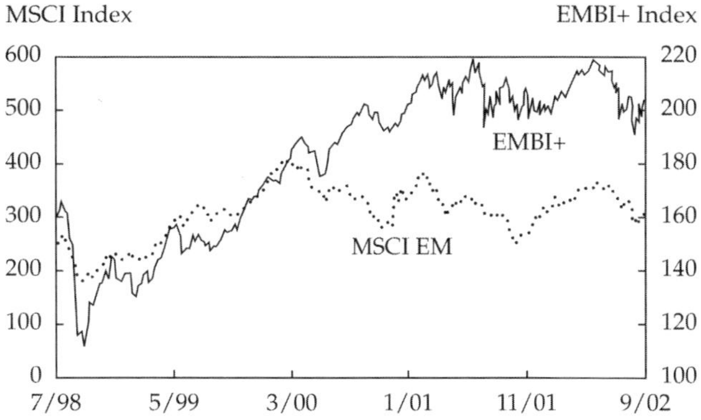

Source: Based on data from Morgan Stanley Dean Witter, J.P. Morgan Chase, and Bloomberg Financial Markets.

Three factors explain the consistent outperformance of emerging market bonds versus equities, a trend that is likely to continue. First, emerging market governments tend to react quickly to negative economic shocks. They cut spending and raise taxes and interest rates—actions that negatively affect private corporations, so that government debt problems are solved at the expense of creating a more challenging operating environment for corporations. Second, emerging market governments have significant international reserves: South Korea has more than US$100 billion; Russia, US$45 billion; Mexico, US$36 billion; and even Brazil, US$37 billion. Most corporations lack such shock absorbers. Third, during crises, emerging market governments have access to lenders of last resort that are located outside their national borders: the International Monetary Fund (IMF), the World Bank, and similar institutions. In the case of emerging market corporations, their emergency support typically lies within the borders of their home country, which is often also experiencing similar funding-related problems.

Emerging market debt also offers significant diversification benefits, as shown in **Table 2**. (Table 2 refers to the same indexes referenced in Figure 1.) The recent correlation of the asset class with U.S. government bonds has been low, and the correlations with U.S. high-yield bonds and equities have been only 40–50 percent.

The ugly side of this asset class is volatility. A simple way to see volatility is to examine annual returns, as shown in **Figure 4**. Since 1991, three negative-return years have occurred: 1994's Mexican peso crisis and related U.S. market sell-off; 1998's Russian default and the Long-Term Capital Management debacle; and 2001's Argentine default. Yet despite Argentina, 2001's negative return was not large, and in 2002, despite the negative global market environment—a major equity market sell-off, heightened global risk aversion, and slower economic growth—total returns were slightly positive through 30 August.

Within the past year, however, enormous volatility has occurred. **Figure 5** shows the three-month rolling volatility of the EMBI+ returns. Volatility decreased after the Russian crisis and remained low during the Argentine crisis but increased significantly during 2002. This "Achilles heel" of the asset class has caused many investors to turn away.

Measuring volatility alone, however, is not sufficient. The real consideration should be volatility-adjusted returns. The data in **Table 3** show the annual return per unit of volatility from 1993 through 2001 for emerging market debt, emerging market equities, and U.S. high-yield bonds. Clearly, emerging market debt offered better returns per unit of volatility and equal or better diversification (for a U.S. equity investor).

As a result of such risk-adjusted performance, more and more investors are becoming interested in emerging market debt. The proportion of emerging market countries rated as investment grade has risen to about 40 percent of countries in the emerging market indexes. The weightings structure across investor segments has become much more balanced, and the average portfolio weighting of this asset class is rising. Commercial banks have been replaced by crossover and local investors as the primary investors in emerging market debt. It follows that emerging market debt is an appropriate asset class for core-plus mandates. It can also be included in "alternative" allocations and serve as a complement to high-yield bonds and emerging market equities.

Investing Process for Emerging Market Debt

This section describes PIMCO's approach to investing in emerging market debt. Our process has four critical elements: menu philosophy, three-pronged analysis, range of products, and risk management.

Table 2. Diversification Benefits of Various Asset Classes for Three-Year Period Ending 31 August 2002

	3-Year Correlation Matrix					
	EMBI/EMBI+	LBAG	LBHY	S&P	Nasdaq	MSCI EM Free
EMBI/EMBI+	100.0%	17.4%	51.4%	41.3%	47.8%	69.2%
LBAG	17.4	100.0	2.1	–25.9	–19.4	2.5
LBHY	51.4	2.1	100.0	45.6	48.2	19.8
S&P	41.3	–25.9	45.6	100.0	76.5	82.6
Nasdaq	47.8	–19.4	48.2	76.5	100.0	81.9
MSCI EM Free	69.2	2.5	19.8	82.6	81.9	100.0

Source: Based on monthly index returns from Lehman Brothers, Bloomberg Financial Markets, and Morgan Stanley Dean Witter.

Figure 4. Total Annual Return for EMBI and EMBI+, 1991–2002

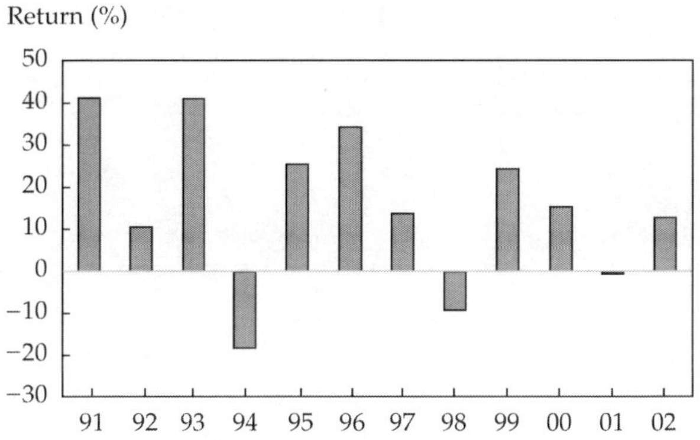

Note: 2002 data as of December.

Source: Based on data from Bloomberg Financial Markets, Morgan Stanley Dean Witter, and Lehman Brothers.

Figure 5. Three-Month Volatility of Emerging Market Debt Index Returns

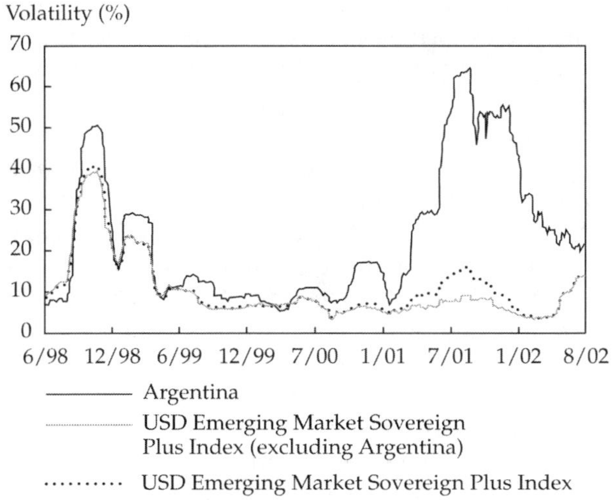

Note: 2002 data as of 30 August.

Source: Based on data from Merrill Lynch.

The Menu Approach. At a restaurant, you do not feel compelled to order every item on the menu. We believe investors should choose emerging market bonds just as they would choose items from a menu—by staying away from certain instruments even if they are on the menu (i.e., in the index).

Three-Pronged Analysis. We measure the fundamentals of each country in our core portfolio. First of all, each credit should make sense on a stand-alone basis; that is, the issuer should have the economic and sociopolitical conditions necessary to strengthen its ability and willingness to pay. Second, each country must have a supportive external environment; it must live in an acceptable neighborhood. For example, one's view of Mexico should depend to some extent on what one thinks of the United States, Mexico's next-door neighbor. The third prong of analysis refers to "market technicals." The Russian and Asian crises taught investors respect for such technicals. An understanding of the fundamental relationships between various global segments and primary investors is crucial because, if ignored, an event in one market may contaminate holdings in another, even if the contaminated holdings are geographically removed from the problem market.

We analyze and choose core allocations with all three of these criteria in mind to ensure that the high-yield potential of the class is accompanied by some level of downside protection. The goal is to avoid accidents, because this asset class tends to have huge accidents, not small ones.

Country fundamentals. We look at a number of factors that ultimately determine the willingness and the ability of governments to pay their debt obligations:

- *State of the economy.* A contracting economy will not generate enough revenues for debt repayment.
- *Fiscal and monetary policies.* Policies must be responsible and sustainable.
- *Debt dynamics.* Even if current economic management is excellent, the debt load from the past may prove to be overwhelming.
- *International reserve cushions.* These cushions must be sufficient to act as shock absorbers in the event that markets are closed to debt rollovers.
- *Contingent funding and policy responses.* Emerging market countries are exposed to shocks, and their creditworthiness depends on their ability to absorb those shocks. Contingency and actual funding and internal policy reaction functions help determine the ability to repay during crises.
- *Sociopolitical developments.* Populations must be willing and able to accept short-term sacrifices that are part of emerging markets' ability to react to unanticipated negative shocks.

Willingness to pay is a critical factor, but it is influenced by policy and political issues, particularly policy responses and ongoing sociopolitical developments. These characteristics should be assessed not only from headquarters but also from within the country.

External environment. Based on input from PIMCO's cyclical and secular forums, we analyze the affect of changes in the global economy on the

Table 3. Correlation and Volatility-Adjusted Returns for Various Asset Classes, December 1993–December 2001

Asset Class	Annualized Return[a]	Cumulative Return[a]	Annualized Volatility of Monthly Returns	Return per Unit of Volatility[b]	Correlation with Lehman Brothers Aggregate Bond Index	Correlation with S&P 500
EMBI+	9.08%	100.44%	18.51%	0.49	0.20	0.55
MSCI EM Free (EM equity)	–6.41	–41.15	24.60	–0.99	–0.08	0.68
LBHY	5.47	53.12	6.51	0.22	0.31	0.53

[a]Returns do not reflect any deduction of fees or expenses.
[b]Return per unit of volatility is calculated by dividing annualized return by annualized monthly volatility of return.

Source: Based on data from PIMCO, J.P. Morgan Chase, and Lehman Brothers.

emerging market world, with an emphasis on income and price effects. We examine the implications of the global economy for commodity prices and global interest rates. We try to answer the question of whether specific emerging markets will gain or lose as a result of prevailing global economic conditions (i.e., global demand, international interest rates, commodity prices, and so forth). Also, many emerging countries do not yet have institutions strong enough to withstand great external shocks. So, a critical step is to determine if an anchor of some form exists for the country under evaluation, such as U.S. support for Mexico.

- *Technicals*. Investors need to assess the following technical indicators: investor risk appetite, flow of funds, leverage in the system (i.e., will leverage in the system amplify volatility?), marginal price setters, and relative value. Relative value is particularly important. Comparisons should occur between countries, within countries (sovereign versus corporate), and between instruments (e.g., Brady bonds versus global bonds). We believe that it is also critical to assess emerging market debt relative to both complementary and competing asset classes (i.e., investment-grade and high-yield bonds).

Range of Products. The third element of our overall approach is the range of products—tactical and strategic. Many products are available, and they have different characteristics and different objectives in terms of overall investment strategy. Investors may choose to consider a particular subset of emerging markets (e.g., the less volatile, higher-rated countries) or to approach the asset class from a broader perspective. They can also blend their emerging market exposure with complementary asset classes in a fashion that modifies the expected Sharpe ratio.

Risk Management. The final element of our approach is risk management. No single good risk measure exists, and both qualitative and quantitative measures are important.

Our quantitative methods are based on PIMCO's standard portfolio management tools, including measures of interest rate duration and duration-weighted exposure, tracking-error and information ratio, and compliance with portfolio guidelines. These measures are supplemented by proprietary analytics, with particular emphasis on avoiding "black holes." These complementary metrics include country overweights/underweights, country betas, spread duration and duration-weighted exposure, and attribution analysis.

Our qualitative methods amount to continuous, formal monitoring of credit fundamentals and market developments and include a daily note, a weekly look ahead, and monthly and quarterly assessments.

Every day, we independently (i.e., without simply following the guidance of sell-side analysts) look at the new data for each emerging market country and reach an assessment that is checked against our own priors and what the experts are saying on the Street. Our daily notes are important because, given informational inefficiencies, conditions can change quickly in this asset class.

Current Market Conditions

Emerging market debt has overcome the 1997–98 crises and the 2001 Argentine situation but experienced a sell-off after a strong first quarter in 2002. **Figure 6** shows the EMBI+ spread over U.S. Treasuries. Spreads have widened since April 2002 as a result of global risk aversion and internal country politics.

Global risk aversion has increased significantly, which has affected emerging market debt in two ways. The first effect is that commercial banks have exited credit markets in emerging countries, partly in reaction to the deterioration in their share prices and partly from a desire to clean up their balance sheets.

Figure 6. EMBI+ Spread over Treasuries

Source: Based on data from J.P. Morgan Chase.

Banks exited the markets by refusing to renew credit lines as well as by purchasing aggressive credit default protection. Because banks have been massive buyers of credit default protection, their actions cause the cash market to suffer.

The second effect of changing global risk aversion is that bargain hunters, who would normally step in, are waiting on the sidelines. In times of great uncertainty in economic and international affairs, the "animal spirits," in Keynes' phrase, tend to diminish. The state of the U.S. economy, whether it is in recovery or heading for a double-dip recession, is unclear. Also, as a result of the recent string of corporate and accounting scandals, the "referees" of the market system—the analysts, accountants, rating agencies, and regulators—are being scrutinized. Furthermore, problems in international affairs, such as terrorism threats and a potential war with Iraq, create additional anxiety. As a result, many investors are waiting to see how these situations will evolve before investing in risky emerging market debt.

The other major reason for widening spreads is internal politics. Emerging market countries experience the ebb and flow of political cycles, and the current cycle is one of the politically noisiest that I have observed in 20 years of covering emerging market debt. The reason political noise is so important is that it can amplify market inefficiency.

George A. Akerlof of the University of California at Berkeley was awarded a share of the 2001 Nobel Prize in economics for his paper "The Market for Lemons: Quality Uncertainty and the Market Mechanism."[3] This work deals generally with asymmetric information in markets, but his simple example applies to used cars. Suppose I am trying to sell you my car. I have serviced it regularly and have treated it well and am offering a vehicle that is in excellent condition. But you have heard about other sellers fiddling with their odometers, reconditioning their cars, and so forth. With such noise in the system, I have no way of convincing you that my car is better. The informational asymmetry is too great. You cannot know the actual condition and history of my car, so you will likely ask for—and often get—my car at a price that values it as a lemon, even though it is not.

A similar situation is at work in emerging market debt. Emerging market debt trades like used cars. Bad information (a negative shock) in one market leads to investor concerns in many other markets. Once investors are surprised by one lemon in their portfolios, they begin to worry about other lemons waiting to be discovered. With a big negative shock, everything can start trading at lemon prices. Of course, sometimes positive shocks cause all markets to bounce up, as in January 2000, when the Federal Open Markets Committee surprisingly cut the target rate by 50 bps, but such positive shocks are rare.

The Outlook

Looking ahead, the answers—as yet unknown—to several critical questions pertaining to the external environment and individual country fundamentals will shape the future of emerging market debt.

External Environment. Two questions dealing with the external environment for emerging market debt are crucial to the ability of the asset class to contribute to the future performance of fixed-income portfolios. The first question is: When will global risk aversion lessen, including the curtailment of the generalized bank retrenchment from credit markets? Commercial banks have exited emerging markets a few times in the past 20 years but always reenter eventually. Such a retrenchment translates into a balance sheet adjustment that is, by definition, a valuation adjustment. The adjustment stops when balance sheet liabilities are reduced to the desired level. Is this adjustment process currently at its beginning, middle, or end?

The second key external environment question is: What is the true state of the U.S. economy? Typically, during the past couple of years, PIMCO has taken a more negative view than the market consensus. A year and a half ago, we suggested that an argument could be made for not buying U.S. corporates at any price. Today, the market consensus is more negative than we are. People are worried about the economy and the possibility of a double-dip recession, but we believe that the United States is a growing concern. The recovery will not be massive,

[3]*Quarterly Journal of Economics* (August 1970):488–500.

nor will we see a total collapse of aggregate demand. Mortgage refinancing is simply too strong a force for a collapse to occur. For example, a colleague of mine refinanced his home mortgage twice within the past year. He did not take a single penny of equity out but reduced his housing cost by 30 percent—and his disposable income increased accordingly. The refinance phenomenon will likely keep the economy afloat until business investment and fiscal stimulus are reinvigorated.

Individual Country Fundamentals. Even for an investor who is more bullish than we are on the two key elements of the external environment, individual country fundamentals constitute an important test for the period ahead. Can a given emerging market country navigate in a global economy that is not flooded with prosperity? The answer depends on the individual country's growth dynamics, its balance sheet, and its policy reactions. For example, we disinvested from Argentina a year before its December 2001 default because our assessment indicated that the government did not have the ability to provide both growth and financial stability. The government could not explain what circumstances would cause the economy to recover and grow; de facto, it simply promised an "immaculate recovery."

Four questions about individual country fundamentals are critical. The first centers on policy, the second on whether the population can tolerate difficult times, the third on the reserve cushion, and the fourth on whether markets can hold the country hostage by refusing to roll over debt.

Countries that satisfactorily stand up to these criteria will offer relatively low volatility and acceptable yield spreads over investment-grade debt. At the high end of this scale are countries such as Mexico, South Korea, Qatar, and South Africa; at the low end are countries such as Argentina, Turkey, and Venezuela, which face considerable challenges.

Two Key Countries

Two countries present crucial considerations for any investor in emerging market debt at this juncture: Argentina and Brazil.

Argentina. Argentina's debt is currently trading at 25 cents on the dollar and, for some, is attractive at this price—the argument being that countries generally do not disappear and that the recent examples of Russia and Ecuador show that significant recovery value is possible.

The current forces at work in Argentina suggest further downside for Argentine instruments. Unfortunately, we think the situation will only get worse. An external debt problem has turned into a full-blown payment systems problem. The deposits in the banking system are frozen, and the system itself has broken down. Political legitimacy has been lost. Because Argentina has lost all of its economic, financial, and political anchors, the sequence of recovery must begin with regaining political legitimacy. The Argentine government, however, is a long way from convincing citizens of its legitimacy. Until that happens, circumstances will continue to worsen.

Why not simply own Argentine debt and wait for things to improve? The reason is that the other shoe has yet to drop. Argentina runs a high risk of falling into arrears on payments to the international financial organizations, the preferred creditors of the world—the IMF, the World Bank, and the Inter-American Development Bank. Having spent 15 years at the IMF, I know that preferred creditor status is seen as absolutely critical to the functioning of the international community. But once a country falls into payment arrears to its preferred creditors, every dollar that can be generated by that country will go to them. Bondholders' claims are relegated to the back of the line and bond recovery values fall. Argentina is not yet a distressed play, but I believe that time will come.

Brazil. Brazil faces three main questions. First, can a reform process that has been in place for three years continue to gather momentum in the context of slower global growth and a reversal in capital flows? Second, given the political noise surrounding the October 2002 election, the economy suffered blow after blow in terms of depreciation of the currency and widening debt spreads. Is Brazil strong enough to withstand these stresses or has permanent damage been done? Third, will the president-elect defer to the market, upset the market more, or perhaps accept default willingly?

The consensus view has Brazil trading at very low levels. In our view, however, Brazil is in a strong position to succeed and the market has overreacted to political uncertainty and global pressures. Our opinion is based on three facts. First, the capital that has been taken out of the country by commercial banks is being replaced by international financial institutions—the IMF committed US$30 billion, the World Bank allocated another US$600 million, and the Inter-American Development Bank is willing to provide additional loans to Brazil.

Second, a similar overreaction to political change has occurred before in emerging markets—for example, in Mexico in 2000 with the election of Vincente Fox, a total unknown who ended more than 70 years of domination by a single political party. Mexico was a BB credit at that time but is now a solid BBB. This turnaround was possible because Mexico had well-anchored economic institutions. Brazil has similar institutions, and we believe these will provide ongoing strength to the country's economy. Finally, if the president-elect of Brazil seeks to default willingly, he must consider the costs and benefits of defaulting. The costs are clear. Consider the example of Argentina, which cannot even finance exports from the factory to the port because the rule of law has been disrupted. Are there any benefits? In the case of Brazil, most of the debt is internal. Defaulting would destroy Brazil's own banking system, which is an extreme position for a politician to take.

Conclusion

Secular trends for the emerging market debt asset class remain positive. They are anchored by good policies, a growing investor base, and improving information quality. The short-term cyclical outlook now, however, is extremely challenging.

At PIMCO, we believe that with a focus on the fundamentals, investors can identify enough quality credits in this asset class to provide significant return and downside protection. To the extent that political noise is present, the asset class may contribute investment opportunity, not simply downside risk.

Given all the headaches that come with emerging markets, is investing in them worth the effort? My answer is yes, with three qualifications. First, investors must understand emerging market debt's role in the asset allocation process. Second, investors need analytical tools and procedures that will aid them in benefiting from the inefficiencies of the market without taking on undue risk. Finally, an explicit and comprehensive risk management process is vital.

Question and Answer Session

Mohamed A. El-Erian

Question: What is your opinion of Jamaica?

El-Erian: One of the opportunities we missed recently was Jamaica. When the road show came to see us, we felt that there wasn't enough information flow available to follow the country on a consistent and timely basis. This decision was unfortunate because Jamaica has done well.

Question: Does a good benchmark exist for emerging market debt?

El-Erian: A few years ago, we criticized J.P. Morgan Chase & Company, the main provider of emerging market indexes. In our view, the EMBI and EMBI+ Indexes were flawed because of concentration issues. As a country needed more money and issued more debt, its weight in the index would grow, and thus, if the country began to experience payment or general credit problems, the entire index would be undermined. Since then, more diversified indexes have been introduced, such as the EMBI Global and EMBI Global Diversified. Another important improvement is that the methodology for calculating each index is now transparent.

Question: What is your opinion about managing against an index?

El-Erian: We have come to the conclusion that investors must be willing to accept one of two things: a larger tracking error at times or a "blended" benchmark. For example, in 2001, Argentina accounted for 22 percent of the EMBI+. After it became clear that Argentina was heading toward, at best, a price default and, at worst, an actual default, we had to make a choice. We chose to accept *ex ante* tracking error by greatly underweighting Argentina because we believe that credit considerations should override tracking-error considerations.

Question: Can tracking error in this situation be minimized?

El-Erian: Yes. Given the inefficiencies of the asset class, ways exist to minimize tracking error. For example, in Argentina's case, there are bouts of what is called "regional contagion"—times when the whole continent trades as one. The reason for this phenomenon is not because we are all idiots and think that Latin America is one country. Regional contagion happens because the significant inflows and outflows into the Latin funds can make these regional funds the marginal price setters for a period of time. For someone who is worried about a Latin American country defaulting but who has a tracking-error constraint, the solution is to treat the region as a bucket. We constructed a bucket that provided 100 percent downside protection against an Argentine default but allowed partial upside in case Argentina's situation improved and the Latin American region rallied as a result.

Question: What is the right investment horizon for analyzing emerging market debt performance?

El-Erian: We typically think in terms of a three-year cycle, which includes both the downside and upside of the cycle. Our emerging market bond fund has never had a negative three-year period and has outperformed the index for every three-year period since its inception.

Question: What role do bond fundamentals play in emerging market debt?

El-Erian: As the asset class matures and the number of investment-grade countries rises, you better get your duration and yield-curve calls right. In the past, interest rate calls, per se, didn't matter as much as they did in other bond market sectors because emerging market debt used to trade more like equities. Today, the fixed-income characteristics of the asset class are starting to outweigh the equity characteristics, so it is crucial to have cyclical and secular views on both the yield curve and duration before investing in emerging market debt.

New Opportunities in High-Yield Bonds

Kevin J. Perry
Vice President and Portfolio Manager
Loomis, Sayles & Company, LP
Boston

Although recent events—defaults, dismal returns, and negative perceptions about the risks of investing in high-yield bonds—may have created the appearance of crisis in the high-yield market, the market is growing and has remained stable as a percentage of the total bond market. Furthermore, new opportunities in the high-yield market can add substantial value for investors. Leveraged bank loans are a particularly attractive new tool, offering both strategic and tactical advantages.

High-yield bonds are not an ancillary asset class; they still have a role to play in broadly diversified fixed-income portfolios. When a core-plus portfolio is benchmarked against a broad index, as it generally is, high-yield bonds are usually a part of that broad index. They have become a permanent part of the U.S. financial structure and fixed-income portfolios.

The first section of this presentation is a description of the current high-yield market environment and addresses the recent changes in the market and the outlook for the future. New opportunities are available in the high-yield market that can add substantial value in core-plus portfolios. In the second section, I describe one of these opportunities, a new instrument in the high-yield world: leveraged bank loans. I will emphasize how and why adding these instruments to high-yield and core-plus portfolios can increase excess return.

High-Yield World

The recent market environment for U.S. corporate bonds, particularly high-yield bonds, has been tough. From the reports of defaults, dismal returns, and negative press releases regarding the risks of investing in the high-yield market, the pervading view might be that the market has died. But it is still alive, although somewhat bruised. In fact, the high-yield market has grown from slightly more than $100 billion in 1987 to roughly $650 billion, as of 30 June 2002. As a percentage of the total bond market, high-yield bonds have remained relatively stable, decreasing only minimally over the past 15 years. Companies, as always, need capital and continue to issue bonds to meet this need.

Recent Poor Performance. Nonetheless, as **Figure 1** shows, although the entire corporate bond market has been difficult and challenging for the past two years, the high-yield market has been downright depressing. In effect, the cumulative total return of the high-yield market has moved sideways since 1997. So, why should bond managers bother with this market if they are not getting paid for the risk involved with it? This question is particularly relevant when the risk, as measured by volatility, is steadily increasing.

Increasing Volatility, Increasing Risk. A few years ago, the case could be made that the high-yield market had an extremely attractive Sharpe ratio. As **Table 1** shows, the ratio was comparable to that of both the high-grade corporate bond market and the equity market over the 1985–2000 period. But when the time period is extended through July 2002, the ratio drops significantly. This diminishing Sharpe ratio has occurred because both sides of the Sharpe equation were hit: Volatility increased and returns decreased.

The investment manager's challenge is to improve return relative to the risk the client is taking. In "classic" modern portfolio theory, the task is defined as achieving the highest possible Sharpe ratio. In terms of the long-term efficient frontier (1990 through June 2002), as illustrated in Panel A of **Figure 2**, the array of efficient portfolios has a much higher

Figure 1. Cumulative Total Return Comparison for Three Bond Sectors (value of $100 invested from 31 December 1990 to 31 July 2002)

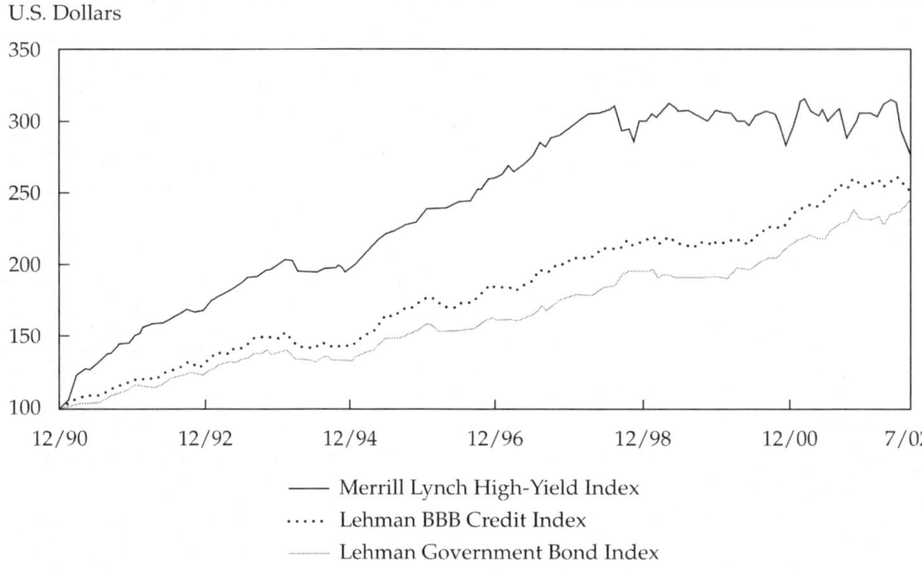

Note: Gross of fees, with all income and dividends reinvested.

Source: Based on data from Lehman Brothers and Merrill Lynch & Company.

Table 1. Sharpe Ratios for Various Asset Classes in Two Periods

Asset Class	1985–2000	1985–2002
10-Year Treasuries	0.13	0.19
Merrill Lynch High-Grade Corporate Index	0.21	0.22
Merrill Lynch High-Yield Index	0.22	0.16
S&P 500 Index	0.22	0.15

Note: The Sharpe ratio is defined as the arithmetic return of the index minus the arithmetic return of the 90-day T-bill divided by the standard deviation of the index return.

Source: Based on Merrill Lynch data.

risk-adjusted return than those on the efficient frontier of the more recent time period (1996 through June 2002) illustrated in Panel B of Figure 2. On the longer-term frontier, the portfolio with the lowest risk has a high-yield allocation of 20–30 percent, but the lowest-risk portfolio on the shorter-term frontier has almost the inverse allocation. The cause of this turnaround is a confluence of several events, not the least of which is the credit cycle (combined with a significant change in high-yield market liquidity). Other exogenous factors are the U.S. economic recession, September 11, and the Russian crisis.

Liquidity in the high-yield market today differs significantly from that of past periods and will not revert to historical levels. Ten years ago, the broker/dealer community truly acted in that capacity by maintaining sizable inventories to meet investors' needs. Today, the Street's high-yield inventory is effectively held in clients' portfolios. Driving this change is the broker/dealer community's use of value at risk (VAR) and other quantitative models to determine the capital allocation to the various trading desks within each firm. For example, increased variability in Nasdaq securities may result in less capital allocated to other market sectors, including high-yield bonds. On some days, the capital allocation to the high-yield desk will be zero. This structural market change will not be reversed. The use of VAR to allocate broker/dealers' risk capital will permanently increase market volatility because the natural buffer of broker/dealer inventory will no longer exist.

"In the long run, we are all dead," as John Maynard Keynes famously said, but for those of us in the bond business, the truth is that in the short run, we can all be fired. Although the long-term returns for the high-yield market have been competitive, the short-term returns relative to the Lehman Aggregate have been absolutely awful. The excess return in the high-yield market has bounced all over the place, with particularly weak returns in 2000 and 2001 relative to other sectors of the market, as shown in **Table 2**. If results are attractive in the long run but terrible

Figure 2. Risk-Adjusted Return for Various Bond Portfolios (annualized rate of return)

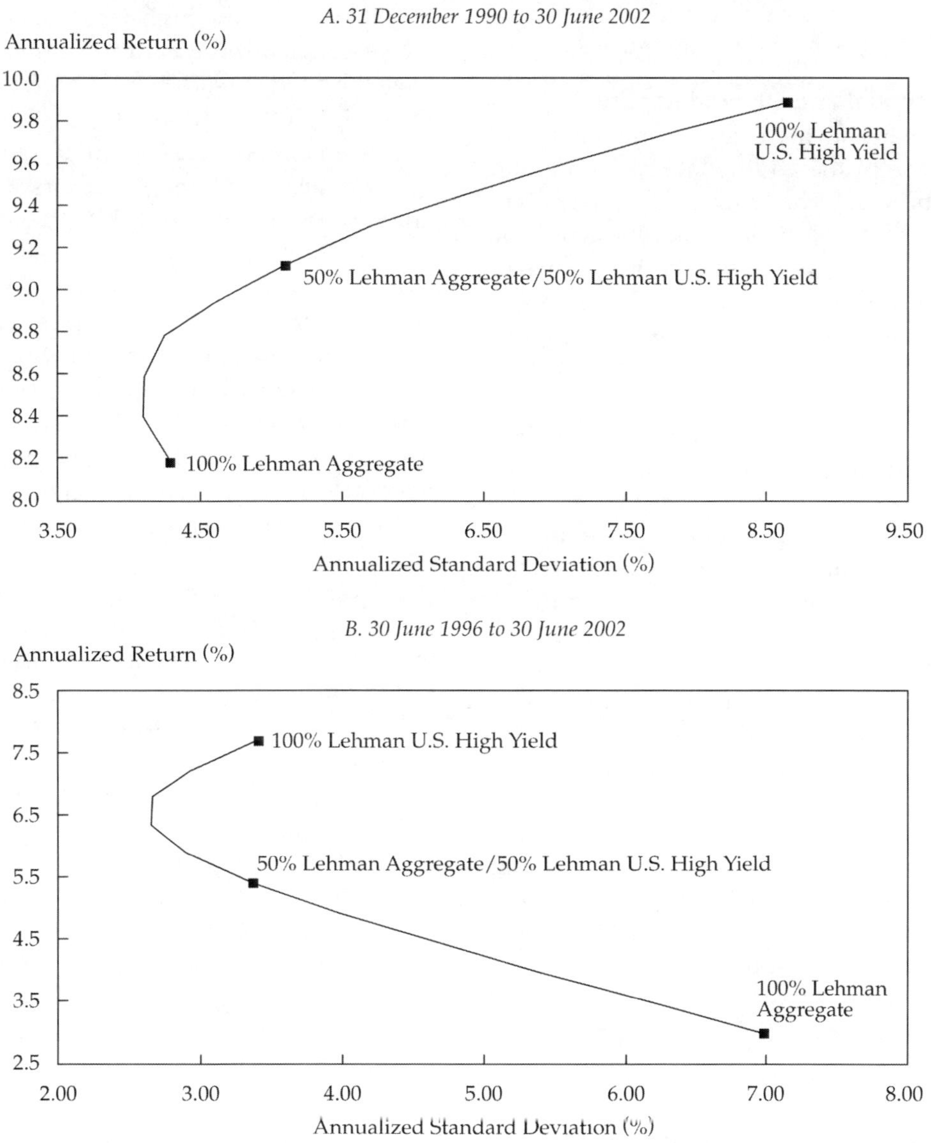

Source: Based on data from Lehman Brothers.

Table 2. Annualized Excess Returns over the Lehman Aggregate Index, 31 December 1993–31 July 2002

Index	1993	1994	1995	1996	1997	1998	1999	2000	2001	2002
Lehman Brothers BBB Credit	12.92%	–3.19%	22.73%	4.02%	11.09%	6.84%	–0.81%	7.41%	10.20%	–1.20%
Lehman Brothers Aggregate	9.75	–2.92	18.48	3.61	9.67	8.68	–0.83	7.12	8.40	5.00
Excess return	3.17	–0.27	4.25	0.41	1.42	–1.84	0.02	0.29	1.80	–6.20
Lehman Brothers High Yield	17.18	–1.16	19.92	11.06	12.83	3.66	1.57	–3.79	5.30	–9.0
Lehman Brothers Aggregate	9.75	–2.92	18.48	3.61	9.67	8.68	–0.83	7.12	8.40	5.0
Excess return	7.43	1.76	1.44	7.45	3.16	–5.02	2.40	–10.91	–3.10	–14.0

Source: Based on data from Lehman Brothers.

in the short run, the real issue for managers is dealing with high volatility, not avoiding low returns. And volatility is not a problem solely associated with the high-yield market; consider the volatility of the Treasury market since 1983, as shown in **Figure 3**.

Return Potential and Diversification. If volatility is a problem in both the Treasury and high-yield markets, why accept the additional risk of a credit downgrade or blowup? The answers lie in the potential for excess return and strong risk diversification in the high-yield market versus the Treasury market.

With high-yield bonds, an investor can diversify along two dimensions—credit exposure and interest rate exposure—to benefit from a diversified risk basket. Treasuries provide only interest rate exposure, and thus, a Treasury-only portfolio is an undiversified risk basket. In mid-2002, credit spreads are wide and high-yield bonds look cheap. In contrast, the Treasury market is not particularly cheap and appears to be bottoming out in terms of rates. Therefore, the high-yield market is relatively more attractive today than the Treasury market in terms of return potential.

The definition of risk for core-plus strategies—or for assembling any diversified portfolio—is covariance. Covariance is a measure that captures the correlation of two variables and is used to calculate the extent to which two variables move together. **Table 3** lists the correlations of high-yield bonds to other bond markets and the S&P 500 Index from 1985 to July 2002. The correlations have remained fairly low over this time period in spite of the tremendous return volatility in recent years. The bottom line is that the risk-reducing potential of adding high yield to a portfolio has remained intact in spite of a tough few years.

Going forward, will managers get paid for taking the extra risk in the high-yield markets arising from increased volatility? **Figure 4** provides some clues. Note the yield spreads between investment-grade (A rated), BBB rated, BB rated, and high-yield (B rated) debt from January 1989 through July 2002. By historical standards, the high-yield market in 2002 is cheap, but because the market is bifurcated, not all sectors are equally cheap. In 1990, the high-yield market was also bifurcated; the financial services and real estate sectors experienced heavy losses while other high-yield sectors did not. The following year, however, the entire high-yield market returned about 40 percent. I do not expect a similarly strong return in 2003 because of structural changes in the market, but nonetheless, at the current level of pricing (very high yields), reversion to the mean should lead to substantial returns.

The future, however, will not be governed totally by this expected reversion to the mean. Another important factor is the change in the behavior of the rating agencies. Their business model has shifted and they are now quicker to react, although they have always reacted quickly in select situations. Now, they are measuring a greater number of variables to produce their ratings and they now generate volatility and bankruptcy predictions using factor models. One concern is that this quicker response time can become a self-fulfilling prophecy. Too quick a downgrade could create bankruptcy conditions instead of merely describing such conditions. The market behavior associated with this change on the part of

Figure 3. Annual Return for 10-Year T-Notes, 31 December 1982 to 31 July 2002

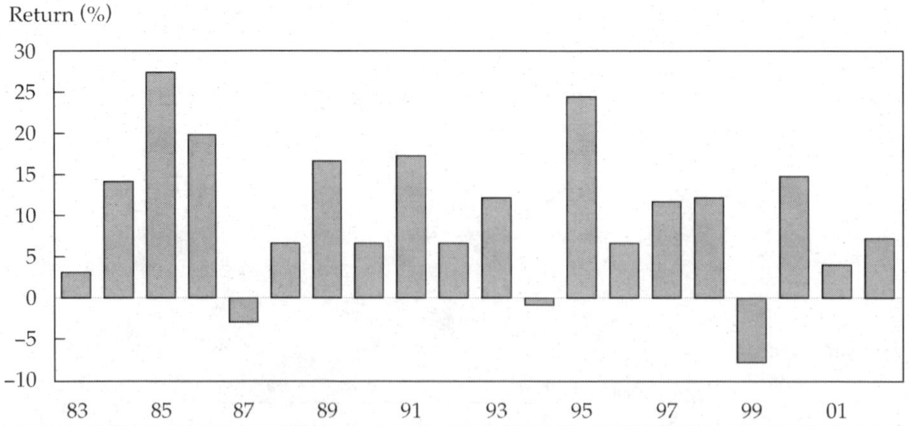

Source: Based on data from Lehman Brothers.

Table 3. Correlations of High-Yield Bonds with Various Asset Classes, 1985–2002

Asset Class	Merrill Lynch High-Yield Index
Merrill Lynch Mortgage	0.33
10-Year U.S. Treasuries	0.34
Merrill Lynch High-Grade Corporate	0.32
S&P 500	0.52

Note: Ending date is 31 July 2002.

Source: Based on Merrill Lynch data.

the rating agencies has not yet worked its way through the system, so the mean reversion that I have forecast will probably not happen in the same way as in previous cycles.

Even with the recent poor market environment, the annualized excess return for the high-yield market has been attractive relative to other market sectors when measured from the beginning of 1991 through July 2002. For example, the Lehman Brothers BB Credit Index had an annualized return over this period of 9.22 percent compared with the Lehman Brothers A Credit Index of 8.49 percent and the 10-year Treasury of 7.60 percent.

Neither the laws of the business cycle nor the laws of the credit cycle have been repealed. Both are (depressingly) alive and well. **Figure 5** shows the corporate bond downgrade-to-upgrade ratio from 1989 through June 2002. Since the last cyclical bottom, the ratio has been increasing in a typical cyclical pattern, and by mid-2002, it had moved virtually off the charts. As the cycle reverses, the ratio should fall and the credit environment should improve, eventually translating into increased returns.

In the high-yield world, returns are negatively correlated with defaults. So, the pattern in **Figure 6** should be no surprise. True to the cyclical pattern in defaults, the current default rate has now returned to the 1990–91 levels of 9–10 percent. I believe the default rate will cycle down again soon, but if defaults remain high, one of two scenarios will occur. Either the high-yield market will disappear—and quickly (because a credit market cannot exist with a 10 percent annual default rate)—or all other credit levels in the capital structure will be repriced, leading to successive rounds of rising yields. The latter scenario would kill the economy, but neither scenario is likely. The most likely scenario is that the economy will improve and the default rate will eventually revert to the mean, which would lead to a narrowing in spreads and higher returns.

High-yield bonds are a significant and growing asset class that offers attractive risk–reward charac-

Figure 4. Yield Spreads by Credit Quality, 1 January 1989–31 July 2002

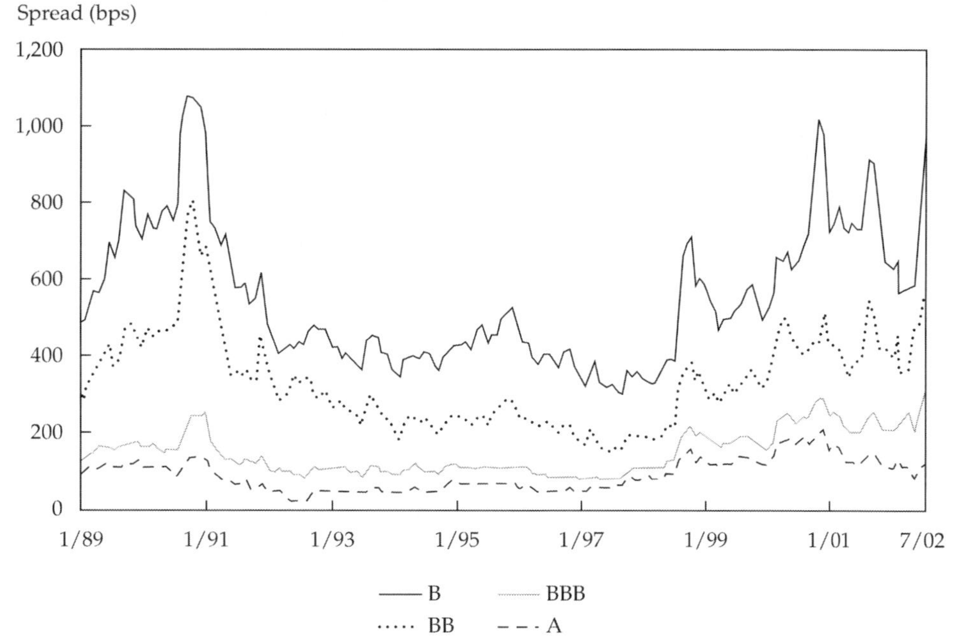

Note: Spreads calculated as the yield to maturity of the respective Lehman Brothers index minus the current 10-year Treasury yield.

Source: Based on data from Lehman Brothers.

Figure 5. Corporate Bond Downgrade-to-Upgrade Ratio, 1989–2002

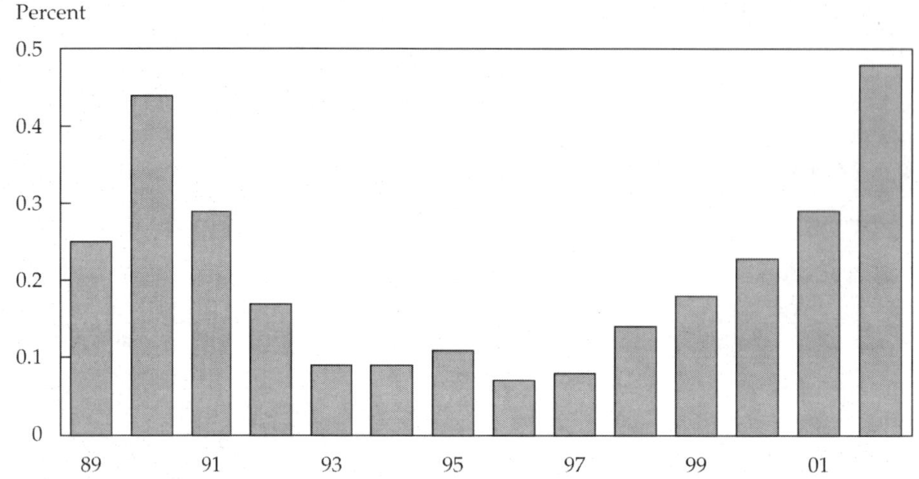

Note: 2002 data as of 30 June 2002.

Source: Based on data from Moody's Investors Service.

Figure 6. Annual Default Rate versus High-Yield Market Return, 1987–2001

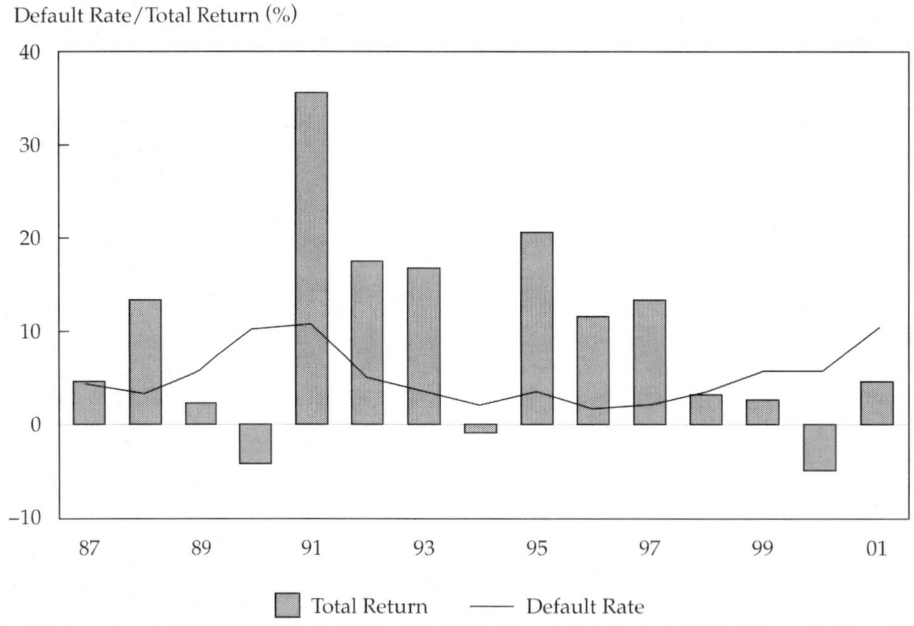

Notes: "Total Return" is the Merrill Lynch High-Yield Master Index annual total return. "Default Rate" is Moody's trailing 12-month speculative-grade-issuer default rate.

teristics and provides compelling diversification benefits, but this asset class is suitable only for experienced managers and investors with long time horizons. In the future, the risk–return picture for high-yield bonds will not be the same as it has been in the past. Volatility will be higher. The inventory in the high-yield market is *your* (the investor's) inventory; the Street is not providing the same liquidity function as it has in the past. Nevertheless, the current market environment offers attractive investment opportunities in the high-yield sector.

New Tool: Bank Loans

To cope with the new reality of higher volatility, fixed-income managers need new tools. A tool that I recommend is leveraged bank loans, which we at Loomis, Sayles & Company view as a subsegment of the high-yield market. Institutions have increasingly found that there are good reasons to invest in bank loans. We call the loans "leveraged" because when we first started to buy them, in the late 1980s, the loans were made to highly leveraged companies. It was the era of the leveraged buyout. In 1987, the average cash flow multiple (the ratio of bank and nonbank debt to earnings before interest, taxes, depreciation, and amortization [EBITDA]) was almost 9, with banks lending about half a company's capital structure. But these loans have consistently improved in credit quality over the years. In 2001, the average cash flow multiple was less than 4 and the ratio of bank debt to EBITDA was down to 2.2. In a reorganization, the bank lender generally will be repaid when the credit exposure is only two times cash flow.

Bank loans are simply loans made by major banks to corporate America. They are not securitized or structured instruments; an investor in a bank loan buys a piece of the original loan. Typically, bank loans are the most senior part of a company's capital structure—junior only to employee wages and taxes.

The rule of thumb for bank loan recoveries has been 80 cents on the dollar, but because a bank lender sits at the top of the capital structure and can usually drive the bankruptcy reorganization process, the bank loan has a good chance of being repaid. In July 2002, Standard & Poor's released a study that, for the first time, accurately examined recovery rates on defaulted debt.[1] S&P deciphered what an investor would truly recover from various types of debt if held through the entire workout period. The median recovery rate for bank loans from 1988 through the end of 2001 was 100 percent. The mean was about 85 percent. Obviously, some borrowers really blow up and are unable to pay back even their most senior lenders. In general, if the bank loan recovery rate is very low, every other lender (including bondholders) will be absolutely crushed. The lesson is that bank loans stand a much better chance for repayment than do related bond issues.

Bank loans are usually secured by the assets (collateral) of the borrower, but the type of collateral is crucial to the true security it provides. The collateral can be illusionary. This problem was seen in the early 1990s when the collateral securing leveraged financial services firms could be taken by the federal government, leaving the lenders empty-handed. More recently, telecommunications companies have proved that assets pledged as collateral are only as good as the business plans for using the assets. Debt may be secured, but the value of the collateral will not be very high if the business is nonexistent.

Bank loans are usually protected by tight covenants that are not easily negotiated. If a covenant is violated, the bank can require that the loan be immediately repaid. Typically, a bank loan has more and tighter covenants than bonds, which is good for the investor who chooses to invest in bank loans.

Loan covenants also affect the average life of the bank loan. The average life of a loan is generally stated as 5–12 years based on the specified term. In reality, however, each loan has a number of tranches, with different stated maturities. Loan tranches are not tranches in the sense of mortgage-backed securities. Typical loan tranches would include a short-term revolver, a Term A piece, a longer-term Term B piece, and so on. Most loans are paid off early because of such events as asset sales, covenant violations, and rate changes, and these early payoffs make bank loans an asset class with a typical average life of about 2.5 years.

Another important point is that bank loans are floating-rate obligations that reset frequently. This feature effectively makes bank loans zero-duration instruments, which means that bank loans will reduce total volatility when added to a fixed-income portfolio. The value of a portfolio of loans is not unvarying, but it will not vary as much as a traditional fixed-income portfolio as a result of interest rate changes. The potential to reduce portfolio volatility is a key advantage of bank loans.

Market. We think of bank loans as a subsegment of the high-yield market. The leveraged bank loan market (i.e., the loans that are truly syndicated and available to nonbank investors) consists mostly of BB rated loans. More loans are being rated every year, but most hover around BB, which is one reason we consider this sector to be part of the high-yield world.

The bank loan asset class is relatively new to institutional investors, who began adding it to their portfolios in the late 1980s. But just because this class is new to institutional portfolios does not mean that the market segment is new. As **Figure 7** shows, the market for leveraged loans is larger than the high-yield market and growing rapidly. This kind of growth does not happen without a good reason, and in this case, the growth has occurred because banks have changed their behavior. Banks now view their portfolios as precisely that—portfolios. They buy and

[1]Roger J. Bos, CFA, Kevin Kelhoffer, and David Keisman, "Ultimate Recovery in an Era of Record Defaults," Standard & Poor's (30 July 2002).

Figure 7. Historical Growth of Leveraged Loan Market, 1989–2001

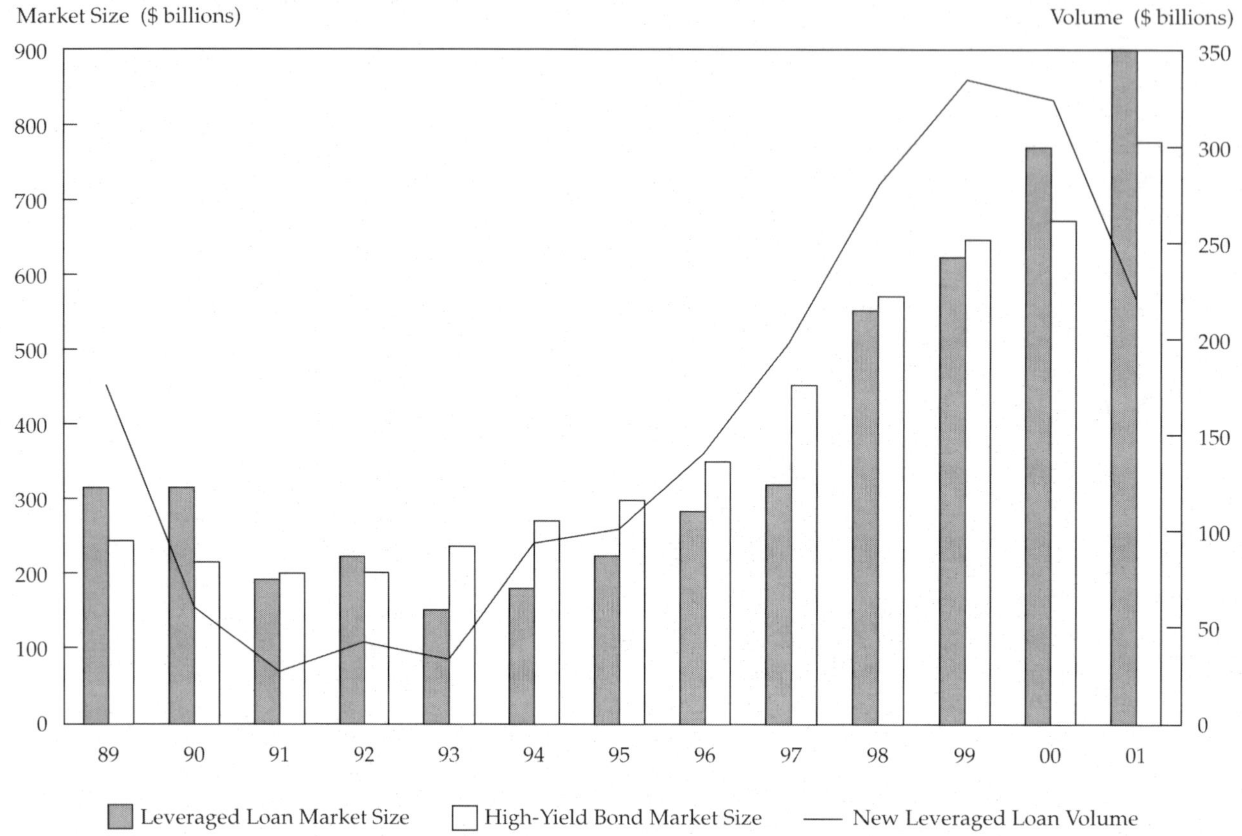

Note: Leveraged loan data are for the syndicated BB rated market.

Source: Based on data from J.P. Morgan Chase & Company and Credit Suisse First Boston.

sell rather than simply hold. In the deals that we buy, the originating bank is typically the largest holder. The originating bank maintains its position both as an investment and as a mechanism to manage the relationship with the borrower. In our view, this behavior strengthens the security of our investment.

Liquidity in this market is significantly higher than it has been in the past. In addition to the banks, every major broker/dealer firm has a trading desk for syndicated bank loans. As **Table 4** shows, for each of the past two years about $120 billion in bank loans has been traded in the secondary market. In 2000, over three-quarters of the loans traded were valued above 90 percent of par value (par loans), with the balance valued below 90 percent of par value (distressed loans). The proportion of distressed loans traded increased in 2001 from 2000 to nearly a third of the total value traded. In coming years, I expect the percentage of distressed loans traded to decrease as the default rate returns to a more normal level. The improvement in liquidity has been dramatic over the years and is primarily attributable to two factors: standardization and transparency.

Table 4. Secondary Loan Volumes, 1994–2001 (billions)

Year	Par	Distressed
1994	$13.0	$ 7.8
1995	25.6	8.2
1996	34.4	6.6
1997	53.5	8.3
1998	58.5	8.8
1999	69.5	7.1
2000	103.1	25.8
2001	75.9	41.8

Note: Generally, par loans are those that trade at or above 90 percent of face and distressed loans are those that trade at less than 90 percent. These classifications vary significantly, however, within the industry.

Source: Based on data from Credit Suisse First Boston and Portfolio Management Data.

The standardization of transactions has led directly to improved bank loan market liquidity. The Loan Syndication and Trading Association has done a great job in this area. To buy a bank loan, a manager simply executes an assignment to the bank loan, which is a two-page, standardized agreement. Transacting no longer requires big meetings in New York City to produce closing documents.

The second major reason for the improved liquidity in the bank loan market is transparency. Transparency of pricing has improved dramatically. Ten years ago, the pricing of a bank loan portfolio required fair-value pricing, which is a dreadful chore if done correctly. Today, a manager can probably price more than 95 percent of a leveraged bank loan portfolio in the same way high-yield bonds are priced. Several pricing services poll a number of broker/dealers to obtain the latest leveraged loan bid and ask prices, aggregate the quoted prices, and provide customers with a price estimate based on the clients' preferred pricing methodology.

More than 78 institutions—including Loomis Sayles, Van Kampen, and Fidelity—are active in this market, managing more than 213 various investment vehicles. Bank loans back guaranteed investment contracts and are included in the core portfolios of insurance companies. They are also held by mutual funds and are used in structured products, total return products, buy-and-hold products, yield products, and so on. This is an active market with diverse participants.

Role in a Portfolio. Table 5 provides summary statistics for the performance of various asset classes and U.S. inflation from 1992 through 2001.[2] Note, on the bottom line, the final three columns for the Credit Suisse First Boston Leveraged Loan Index. Over this long period of time, leveraged bank loans had the highest Sharpe ratio of all asset classes at 1.02, with 10 positive return years and no negative years (as compared with 8 positive years and 2 negative years

[2] See Appendix for asset class descriptions.

Table 5. Summary Statistics for Various Assets, 1992–2001

Asset	Geometric Mean Annual Return	Arithmetic Mean Annual Return	Annual Volatility[a]	Return/Risk[b]	Highest Annual Return	Lowest Annual Return	Annual Median Return	Number Positive Return Periods	Number Negative Return Periods	Sharpe Ratio[c]
U.S. 30-day T-bill	4.56%	4.56%	0.32%	14.09%	5.89%	2.90%	4.77%	10	0	–0.44
U.S. Intermediate Government	6.73	6.83	4.61	1.46	16.80	–5.14	9.29	8	2	0.46
U.S. Long-Term Government	8.73	9.08	8.87	0.98	31.67	–8.96	10.56	7	3	0.49
Merrill Lynch Mortgage	7.19	7.24	3.23	2.23	16.99	–1.56	7.31	9	1	0.79
Merrill Lynch High-Grade Corp.	7.80	7.91	4.86	1.61	21.23	–3.34	9.13	8	2	0.66
Lehman Brothers AAA Corp. Bond Index	7.62	7.73	4.97	1.53	21.41	–3.64	10.55	8	2	0.61
S&P 500 Index	12.93	14.03	15.87	0.81	37.43	–26.22	15.52	8	2	0.59
S&P/Barra Growth Index	12.28	13.44	16.22	0.76	42.16	–29.17	14.52	8	2	0.54
S&P/Barra Value Index	12.31	13.77	18.28	0.67	36.99	–23.53	13.70	8	2	0.50
Wilshire 5000 Index	13.10	14.16	15.55	0.84	36.45	–26.69	16.25	7	3	0.61
Credit Suisse First Boston Conv. Securities	11.07	11.99	14.42	0.77	42.36	–17.05	15.39	7	3	0.50
MSCI EAFE Index	4.76	5.94	15.94	0.30	32.95	–33.48	7.21	7	3	0.08
J.P. Morgan Emerging Markets Bond Index Fixed Rate	15.45	17.01	18.99	0.81	48.99	–25.69	13.63	8	2	0.65
Gold	–2.35	–1.69	11.69	–0.20	17.68	–21.68	–1.33	4	6	–0.55
U.S. Inflation	2.51	2.51	0.71	3.53	3.39	1.61	2.68	10	0	–3.08
Credit Suisse First Boston High-Yield Index	7.88	8.08	6.54	1.21	19.68	–5.66	7.90	8	2	0.52
Credit Suisse First Boston Leveraged Loan Index	7.02	7.05	2.29	3.06	11.17	2.15	7.12	10	0	1.02

[a] Annual volatility is the standard deviation of monthly returns.

[b] Risk is annual volatility; return is geometric mean annual return.

[c] The Sharpe ratio is defined as the arithmetic return of the index minus the arithmetic return of the 90-day T-bill divided by the standard deviation of the index's return.

Source: Based on data from Credit Suisse First Boston and Ibbotson Associates.

for the high-yield bond index, which had a Sharpe ratio of 0.52). In other words, bank loans have provided consistent positive returns with little volatility. Loan returns will not be positive in all quarters, but this period included only three negative quarters (not contiguous). For the long-term period (1992–2001), the results were very impressive.

The factors that led to the leveraged loan performance demonstrated in Table 5 still exist today. Banks still lend less than 50 percent of the capital structure of a company. The loans are still secured and still have tight covenants. And as long as bankers continue to be bankers, the odds are that they will continue to lend money on a secured basis at favorable rates to enhance their bottom line.

In risk–reward terms, leveraged bank loans tend to live in a favorable place, with high returns relative to their risk, as shown in **Figure 8**. The reason is their fundamental arithmetic: They are short term, have essentially zero duration, and have low covariance with other assets.

This very favorable standing does not occur if the asset has high covariance with another asset. Covariance has only three components—the variance of the first asset, the variance of the second asset (in this case, bank loans), and the correlation between the two. Bank loans are inherently a low-variance asset class, so the only other issue is correlation.

Correlations between bank loans and other assets are low across the board, as shown in **Table 6**. Except for the high-yield market, correlations range from a low of –0.13 to a high of 0.13. Bank loans are most highly correlated with high-yield bonds. This high correlation is not surprising because BB rated bank loans essentially represent money lent to B rated high-yield companies. Even so, the correlation is only 0.39. Because the owner of a bank loan is at the top of the borrower's capital structure (above unsecured bonds), the loan is very likely to be repaid, making the inherent duration of the loan zero. Thus, adding bank loans to a fixed-income portfolio can significantly improve the return per unit of risk.

Conclusion

Leveraged bank loans, a relatively new tool for institutional portfolio managers, make sense as additions to institutional portfolios—high-yield bonds and/or core-plus—because of their low correlations with other assets and their low volatility. They have both strategic and tactical advantages.

Strategically, a 20–30 percent allocation to bank loans in either medium-investment-grade or high-yield portfolios can improve both the Sharpe ratio and the tracking error of the portfolio.

Figure 8. Risk–Return Characteristics of Various Assets, 1992–2002

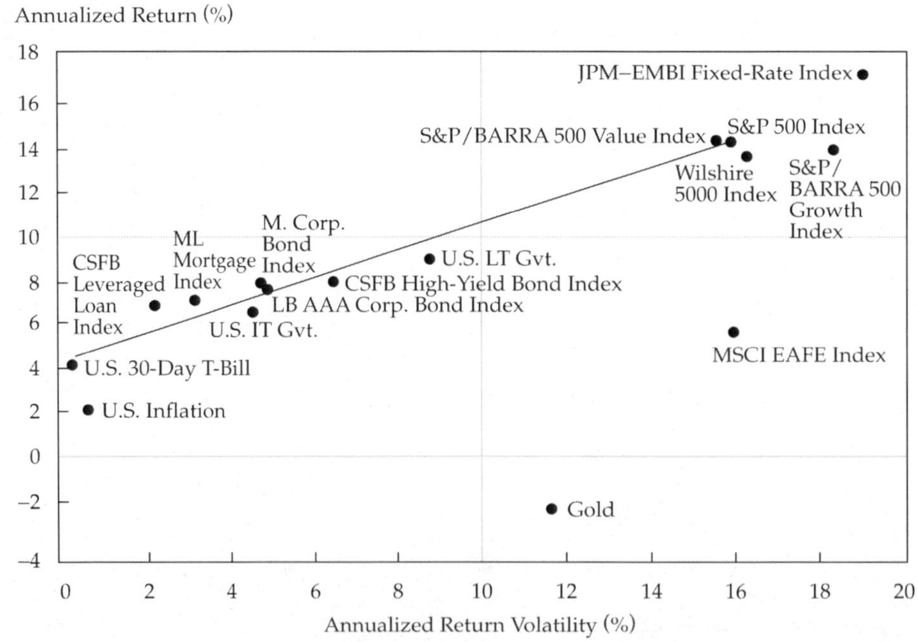

Notes: 2002 data are through the second quarter. Credit Suisse First Boston Leveraged Loan Index outperformance is 146 bps over the market line.

Source: Based on data from Credit Suisse First Boston and Ibbotson Associates.

Table 6. Correlation of Bank Loans with Other Assets

U.S. 30-day T-bill	–0.09
U.S. Intermediate Gvt.	–0.13
U.S. Long-Term Gvt.	–0.04
Merrill Lynch Mortgage	–0.07
Merrill Lynch Corp.	0.02
Lehman Brothers AAA Corp.	–0.03
Credit Suisse First Boston Conv. Securities	0.13
S&P 500	0.08
S&P/Barra 500 Growth	0.03
S&P/Barra 500 Value	0.12
Wilshire 5000	0.10
J.P. Morgan Emerging Bonds Index Fixed Rate	0.02
MSCI EAFE	0.02
Gold	–0.07
U.S. Inflation	–0.08
Credit Suisse First Boston High Yield	0.39

Tactically, bank loans are a valuable arrow in the quiver of the portfolio manager. When analyzed against the Merrill Lynch High-Yield Index during the difficult credit periods—September 1997 to October 1998, April 1999 to December 2000, and May 2001 to December 2001—bank loans outperformed high-yield bonds in every single period. Adding bank loans to the high-yield bond allocation also lowers the overall volatility of the high-yield credit sector. This enhancement is important for a core or core-plus portfolio that has restrictions on the amount that can be allocated to the high-yield asset class. Bank loans help protect high-yield returns.

Tactically, bank loans are also helpful for the manager of an investment-grade portfolio. Adding bank loans to an investment-grade portfolio will improve returns in rising interest rate environments. When rates rise, interest payments on leveraged bank loans reset frequently at higher levels. In the up-rate period from January 1994 to November 1994, the Lehman Aggregate returned about –4.9 percent and bank loans returned about 6.0 percent. In the up-rate period from January 1996 to March 1997, the Lehman Aggregate returned about 1.9 percent and bank loans returned about 7.5 percent. Finally, in the up-rate period from September 1998 to January 2000, the Lehman Aggregate's total return was –0.6 percent and bank loans' total return was 4.1 percent.

The high-yield asset class is a valuable element in fixed-income portfolios because of its diversification (risk-reducing) and excess return potential. The high-yield asset class subset of leveraged bank loans improves on this positive risk-adjusted return by contributing a volatility-dampening effect and consistent positive returns. The basic criterion for evaluating leveraged bank loans, however, is the credit decision, and firms must be staffed appropriately to make it. Bank loans are a very useful addition to high-yield and core-plus portfolios in an increasingly volatile market environment.

Appendix. Asset Class Descriptions[3]

Credit Suisse First Boston (CSFB) Convertible Securities. This index serves as a standard of comparison and measurement of market opportunities for institutional convertible fund managers. This index is calculated monthly and is market-value weighted. The inclusion criteria for domestic convertible bonds and convertible preferred stocks are an S&P rating of B– or greater, market capitalization of $50 million or greater, a minimum of 500,000 shares outstanding, a minimum issue size of $50 million, and no contingent convertibility features. For dollar-denominated euro convertibles issued by U.S.-based companies, the minimum market capitalization is $100 million. The CSFB securities department may also include securities that meet all of the above criteria but do not have a rating by S&P. The index is rebalanced annually.

CSFB High Yield. This index is designed to mirror the investable universe of the U.S.-dollar-denominated high-yield debt market (rated 5Bs or lower; minimum $75MM outstanding; publicly registered or 144(a); no floating rate or convertible debt). If an issuer has more than two issues outstanding, only the two most liquid are included in the index. Issues within one year of maturity are removed from the index. Fallen angels must "season" for three months before inclusion. Energy high-yield bonds, defensive high-yield bonds, cyclical high-yield bonds, BB rated bonds, B rated bonds, and CCC rated bonds are subsectors of the CSFB High-Yield Index. Construction rules for these subsectors mirror those of the CSFB High-Yield Index.

CSFB Leveraged Loan. This index is designed to mirror the investable universe of U.S.-dollar-denominated leveraged loans (rated 5Bs or lower or carrying spreads of LIBOR plus 125 bps or higher). Tenor must be one year or longer; only funded term loans are included, and loans are removed at upgrade to investment grade, maturity, refinancing, or work-out.

[3]Generally, the information regarding bank loans refers only to U.S.-dollar-denominated loans. The information regarding bank loans for which the data source is Standard & Poor's excludes hybrids, as well as all left and right agent commitments (including administrative, syndication, and documentation agent as well as arranger).

Gold. The index returns are calculated from month-end closing prices, expressed in dollars per troy ounce. Total returns are equal to the change in price from month-end to month-end. The data source is the *Wall Street Journal*, London p.m. closing price.

J.P. Morgan Emerging Markets Bond Index Fixed Rate. The J.P. Morgan Emerging Markets Bond Index is a total return index that tracks the traded market for dollar-denominated sovereign restructured bonds (Brady Bonds). The index is market-capitalization weighted, fully invested, and rebalanced monthly.

Lehman Brothers Aggregate Index. The Lehman Brothers Aggregate Index represents securities that are U.S. domestic, taxable, and dollar denominated. The index covers the U.S. investment-grade fixed-rate bond market, with index components for government and corporate securities, mortgage pass-through securities, and asset-backed securities. These major sectors are subdivided into more specific indexes that are calculated and reported on a regular basis.

Lehman Brothers Government Bond. The Lehman Brothers Government Index includes Treasuries (public obligations of the U.S. Treasury that have remaining maturities of more than one year) and agencies (publicly issued debt of U.S. government agencies, quasi-federal corporations, and corporate or foreign debt guaranteed by the U.S. government).

Lehman Brothers U.S. Credit. The Lehman Brothers U.S. Credit Index includes publicly issued U.S. corporate and specified foreign debentures and secured notes that meet the specified maturity, liquidity, and quality requirements. To qualify, bonds must be U.S. SEC registered. The index also includes both corporate and noncorporate sectors. The corporate sectors are industrial, utility, and finance, which include both U.S. and non-U.S. corporations. The noncorporate sectors are sovereign, supranational, foreign agency, and foreign local government. Included are subordinated issues (provided that other specified criteria are met), securities with normal call and put provisions and sinking funds, medium-term notes (if they are publicly underwritten), 144(a) securities (if they have registration rights), and global issues that are SEC registered. Excluded are structured notes with embedded swaps or other special features, private placements, floating-rate securities, and Eurobonds. The U.S. Credit Index is the same as the former U.S. Corporate Investment Grade Index, which has been renamed as the U.S. Credit Index. The name change was effective as of 1 June 2000 for statistics and as of 1 July 2000 for returns.

Lehman Brothers AAA, AA, A, BBB, BB, B Credit. These indexes are composed of their respective components in the U.S. Credit Index (described above).

Lehman Brothers High Yield. The Lehman Brothers High-Yield Index covers the universe of fixed-rate, non-investment-grade debt. Pay-in-kind bonds, Eurobonds, and debt issues from countries designated as emerging markets (e.g., Argentina, Brazil, and Venezuela) are excluded, but Canadian and global bonds (SEC registered) of issuers in non-EMG countries are included. Original-issue zeros, step-up coupon structures, and 144(a)s are also included. The index includes both corporate and noncorporate sectors. The corporate sectors are industrial, utility, and finance, which include both U.S. and non-U.S. corporations. The Yankee sector was discontinued as of 1 July 2000. The bonds in the former Yankee sector have not been removed from the index but have been reclassified into other sectors. The index excludes structured notes with embedded swaps or other special features, private placements, floating-rate securities, and Eurobonds. Defaulted bonds were formerly included in the index but have been removed from the index as of 1 July 2000.

Merrill Lynch Asset-Backed Securities. This Merrill Lynch-generated total-return index tracks the performance of U.S.-dollar-denominated asset-backed securities that have a fixed coupon, a minimum amount outstanding of $25 million (per tranche), and an investment-grade credit rating. The index is rebalanced on the last calendar day of the month.

Merrill Lynch High-Grade Corporates. This Merrill Lynch-generated total-return index includes investment-grade corporate bonds with ratings of BBB–/Baa3 and better. This index includes fixed-rate, coupon-bearing instruments but excludes floating-rate debt, equipment trust certificates, and Title II securities.

Merrill Lynch High Yield. This unmanaged index consists of fixed-rate, coupon-bearing bonds that have an outstanding par greater than or equal to $50 million and a maturity range greater than or equal to one year and that are less than BBB/Baa3 rated but not in default.

Merrill Lynch Mortgage. This Merrill Lynch-generated total-return index includes the Government National Mortgage Association (GNMA), Federal National Mortgage Association (FNMA), and Federal Home Loan Mortgage Corporation (FHLMC) sectors. The index includes fixed-rate, coupon-bearing instruments, and the amount outstanding in each agency/type/coupon subdivision of the mortgage market must be no less than $200 million at the start and at the close of the performance-measurement periods. It excludes Federal Housing Administration project notes, collateralized mortgage obligations, 1/4 coupon pass-throughs, GNMA IIs, graduated payment mortgages, Mobile Homes, and interest-only and principal-only securities.

MSCI EAFE. This Morgan Stanley Capital International equity index includes equities from Europe, Australia, and the Far East regions. Specific countries included are Australia, Austria, Belgium, Denmark, Finland, France, Germany, Hong Kong, Ireland, Italy, Japan, the Netherlands, New Zealand, Norway, Portugal, Singapore, Spain, Sweden, Switzerland, and the United Kingdom.

S&P 500. Standard & Poor's 500 Index is a readily available, carefully constructed, market-value-weighted benchmark of common stock performance. This index composite includes 500 of the largest stocks (in terms of market value) in the United States.

S&P/BARRA 500 Growth. This index is constructed by dividing the stocks in the S&P 500 Index according to price-to-book ratios. The growth index contains stocks with higher price-to-book ratios than stocks in the value index. On average, growth stocks have higher price-to-earnings ratios, lower dividend yields, and higher historical and predicted earnings growth rates when compared with those of the value index. This index is market-capitalization weighted and is rebalanced semiannually based on its price-to-book ratios and market capitalizations. This index contains approximately 50 percent of the S&P 500 capitalization.

S&P/BARRA 500 Value. This index is constructed by dividing the stocks in the S&P 500 Index according to price-to-book ratios. The value index contains stocks with lower price-to-book ratios than stocks in the growth index. On average, value stocks have lower price-to-earnings ratios, higher dividend yields, and lower historical and predicted earnings growth rates when compared with those of the growth index. This index is market-capitalization weighted and is rebalanced semiannually based on price-to-book ratios and market capitalizations, and it contains approximately 50 percent of the S&P 500 capitalization.

U.S. 30-Day T-Bill. This is a total-return index. Each month, a one-bill portfolio that contains the shortest-term bill having not less than one month to maturity is constructed. To measure the holding-period returns for the one-bill portfolio, the bill is priced as of the last reading day of the previous month-end and as of the last trading day of the current month. The data source is the *Wall Street Journal*.

U.S. Inflation. This total-return index uses the Consumer Price Index For All Urban Consumers (CPI-U), not seasonally adjusted, to measure inflation. This is a monthly total-return index that estimates the most current month by taking the average rate of the previous two months.

U.S. Intermediate Government. This is a total-return index. Using the coupon-accrual method, total returns are calculated as the change in the flat or "and interest" price. The flat price is the average of the bid and ask prices plus accrued coupon. A one-bond portfolio is constructed containing the shortest non-callable bond with a maturity of not less than five years and is "held" for the calendar year. Monthly returns are computed. The data source is the *Wall Street Journal*.

U.S. Long-Term Government. This is a total-return index. To the greatest extent possible, a one-bond portfolio with a term of approximately 20 years and a reasonably current coupon was used each year. The bond was "held" for the calendar year, and monthly returns were computed. Total returns were calculated using the coupon-accrual method and are calculated as the change in the flat or and-interest price. The flat price is the average of the bid and ask prices plus the accrued coupon. The data source is the *Wall Street Journal*.

Wilshire 5000. The Wilshire 5000 Equity Index measures the performance of all U.S.-headquartered equity securities with readily available price data. The market-cap-weighted index is comprised of approximately 6,500 security returns. Dividends are reinvested as of the "ex" dividend date, and the rebalancing of share weights is done on a monthly basis.

Question and Answer Session

Kevin J. Perry

Question: Would you expand on the subject of liquidity in the bank loan market?

Perry: These bonds are not as liquid as investment-grade bonds by any stretch of the imagination and do not trade as if they were, but they are closing in on the high-yield market in terms of liquidity. A number of bank loans are more liquid than high-yield bonds. Ten years ago, these securities traded in multiples of $5 million and $10 million; now, they trade in multiples of $1 million and $2 million.

Question: What is the significance of the rise in the number of distressed loans and should we be investing in them?

Perry: Buying distressed loans is a credit decision. In a bad credit market, you simply have more bad loans, which drop in price. But as I mentioned earlier, a distressed loan doesn't imply that you will get less in terms of recovery. Typically, not a lot of trading occurs in distressed loans because most investors understand that if they hold on to them, they're likely to come out whole. Nevertheless, I have not been recommending the distressed loan part of this market. Rather, I am pitching the asset-allocation characteristics of the par loan part of the market. The performance I have been quoting isn't that of distressed loans, which require different management from par loans. Distressed loans are the ultimate credit decision; you have to look at one loan at a time.

Question: What is the best investment strategy for par loans?

Perry: In order for par loans to add value, you must have a broadly diversified portfolio. Diversification is important because you're not buying bonds at 80 percent of par and expecting to get back to par. The market doesn't have the volatility needed to make up for your credit errors. If you loan money to a few hundred people, some of them are not going to pay you back, so you have to spread the risk by broadly diversifying. You should aim for a portfolio of at least 100 names. With the appropriate credit work, you can easily assemble 100 credits that you like in a reasonable amount of time.

Question: Is there any risk that banks will dump their bad loans on the syndicated loan market?

Perry: First, banks have an incentive to get ancillary business in one form or another from their loans. If they commit fraud when they syndicate their loans, they won't get a second opportunity. But the syndication fees are not the only incentive for straight-shooting; banks also syndicate a percentage of their portfolios for diversification and for the efficient use of their capital.

Second, you have to make your own credit decision and do your own credit work. Just as you wouldn't buy bonds based on a single broker recommendation, you wouldn't buy a bank loan that way either.

Question: Are you seeing more BBB-like credits in the market?

Perry: We are not interested in an investment-grade bank loan because they don't have covenants or security. Investment-grade loans look like signature or "trust me" loans. We have no interest in such loans. We want to know how, when, and what we will get paid back.

Question: Is variability in the covenants increasing?

Perry: The LSTA is trying to standardize credit agreements, but its effort is doomed to failure because neither side of the equation wants it. The banks don't want it because then they would have an undifferentiated product that would be compared solely based on price. The borrowers don't want it because every firm that's borrowing money wants to negotiate its own deal and thinks of itself as special. What you will find is much like what you will see in any prospectus. There are modular segments, so you can find things easily as you're going through the credit agreement. I expect modularity to increase. Variability of covenants will not be greater than in the past, but I don't expect it to be lessened either. The selling point is that banks can add and change covenants as needed, so the status quo is likely to remain.

Question: How can I avoid documentation risk?

Perry: Documentation is, to a large extent, handled by the agent bank, and the risk is much like that associated with a collateralized mortgage obligation. So, you need an appropriate servicing agent. Fortunately, the banks syndicating these loans are all large national banks, such as J.P. Morgan Chase & Company and Citibank. To some extent, you do have the risk of fraud and misrepresentation, but you have recourse to these banks. Of course, you need to keep copies of the documents.

Question: What about the problems of becoming an insider by buying loans?

Perry: First, you don't have to be an insider. Most institutions now have public bank books and separate the restricted information. If they don't, you can certainly have the information scrubbed by legal counsel before it gets to you. At Loomis, we have chosen not to be an insider.

If you are an insider, you have a structural issue, but a well-worn path can be followed. You can simply create the appropriate fire wall or screen. It's not expensive. The only expense is the legal fee to set it up. Once it's up and running, it's like any asset class.

The structural issue to pay attention to with bank loans is the accounting. Making sure the accounting is correct is a greater challenge than the fire wall.

Tax-Savvy Fixed-Income Investing

R.B. Davidson III
Director, Municipal Bonds
Bernstein Investment Research and Management
New York City

Managers can enhance after-tax returns by choosing between municipals and taxable bonds based on the investor's tax rate, harvesting municipal bond losses, and realizing taxable bond gains once they become long term. Often, the best strategy is to invest in both taxable and tax-exempt bonds, exploiting the shifting yield relationships and choosing the sector that offers the best after-tax value. Although performance should be reported and measured on an after-tax basis, the absence of adequate databases makes after-tax analysis of a manager's performance difficult; to adjust for duration differences and capture excess performance, analysts should compare municipal portfolios of similar credit quality with a municipal market return line that spans the maturity spectrum.

Two themes are central to after-tax bond portfolio management: (1) exploiting the market and tax code and (2) broadening the investment universe. This presentation describes how after-tax returns can be boosted simply by choosing between municipals and taxable bonds based on the investor's tax rate, harvesting municipal bond losses, and realizing taxable bond gains once they become long term. After-tax management, however, is more than accounting for income and managing losses and gains. For many portfolios, the best strategy is often to invest in both taxable and tax-exempt bonds, taking advantage of shifting yield relationships and choosing the sector that represents the best after-tax value. Finally, this presentation reviews some of the popular methods used to assess portfolio managers, with a recommendation for using a method that compares manager return with a market return line.

Disclosing Sources and Assumptions

The goal of portfolio management for taxable clients is to maximize after-tax total return consistent with the client's guidelines. After-tax total return is the sum of income earned and the change in valuation less taxes paid (both income and capital gains). To achieve the goal of maximizing after-tax return, portfolio managers estimate *expected* bond returns adjusted for taxes payable on both income and capital gains. As such, historical performance data and tax rates are typically the starting point.

This presentation uses historical performance data for the period from January 1992 through July 2002, a period in which tax rates were fairly constant. Unless stated otherwise, my presentation assumes that the client (an individual taxpayer) is taxed at the federal ordinary income tax rate of 38.6 percent and at a state ordinary income tax rate of 5 percent. For individuals subject to the alternative minimum tax (AMT), an income tax rate of 28 percent is used. The state tax liability is assumed to be deductible in the calculation of the federal tax liability unless the client is subject to the AMT. Short-term capital gains are taxed at the ordinary income tax rate (38.6 percent) and long-term capital gains are taxed at a rate of 20 percent.

Once the after-tax expected return is calculated, the manager can then account for after-tax risk and optimize the portfolio to determine the expected maximum after-tax return.

Exploiting the Givens

Accept the gifts that the market and tax code provide. This instruction sounds both obvious and strange, but a few "free lunches" do still exist in after-tax bond management.

Ordinary Income. Panel A of **Figure 1** shows pretax yield curves for the different sectors (corporate, federal agency, U.S. Treasury, and municipal) of the bond market. The yields shown for corporate bonds are for issuers rated A, and the municipal yields are for issuers rated AAA. Furthermore, my assertion is that the relationships in Figure 1 are the "normal" relationships and are indicative of the expected pretax expected returns available in each sector. The normal relationships were built starting with a base of Treasury yields. Treasury yields for each maturity are the average observed over the period from January 1992 through July 2002. The agency yield curve was constructed by adding the average option-adjusted spread of agencies for the same period to the Treasury yield curve. The corporate yield curve was similarly constructed, but the yields were lowered by the amount of Moody's Investors Service's "transition rate"[1] for each maturity. For example, the short-term yields were reduced by 5 bps and long-term yields were reduced by 31 bps. The municipal yield curve was determined by applying the average ratio of municipal yields to Treasury yields over the stated 10½-year period to each maturity on the Treasury yield curve.

These "normal" relationships offer no surprises. Corporate bonds offer the highest expected return per unit of risk. Without considering taxes, municipals are dominated by Treasuries and agencies across the maturity spectrum.

Once taxes are incorporated, however, the expected return for taxable bonds falls dramatically and municipal bonds dominate across the maturity spectrum for the top tax bracket, as shown in Panel B of Figure 1. In the intermediate range, municipals pick up about 70 bps over Treasuries and about 35 bps over A rated corporate bonds. Based on these data, an individual in the top income tax bracket would not want to consider investing in any fixed-income instrument but municipals.

For lower tax brackets, the choice is less obvious. The normal expected after-tax returns for individuals subject to the AMT are shown in Panel A of **Figure 2**. Municipals dominate in the long maturities (30 bps higher than corporates), but agency and corporate bonds have the highest expected after-tax returns for short maturities (offering about 17 and 28 bps more, respectively, than Treasuries and municipals). No sector clearly dominates in the intermediate range (about a five-year duration).

Relationships in the bond market are dynamic, and the relationship of taxable bond yields to tax-exempt bond yields constantly shifts, resulting in commensurate shifts in the after-tax return advantage, as shown in Panel B of Figure 2. In December 1999, municipal bonds were "expensive" based on historical averages and taxable bonds were "cheap." Thus, at the short end of the yield curve on an after-tax return basis, the taxable market dominated even more dramatically than usual and municipal bonds offered only slightly more income than taxable bonds on the long end. The real change, however, is at the five-year duration point, where agencies and corporates offer considerably more income than municipals. Therefore, it appears that an intermediate fixed-income portfolio should consist almost entirely of agency and corporate bonds. But an even better solution exists. By combining short taxable bonds and long municipals, a manager can build a portfolio with an intermediate duration that has higher after-tax income than is available in any single market, be it

Figure 1. Average Yield of Various Bond Sectors for Investors in Top Tax Bracket, January 1992–July 2002

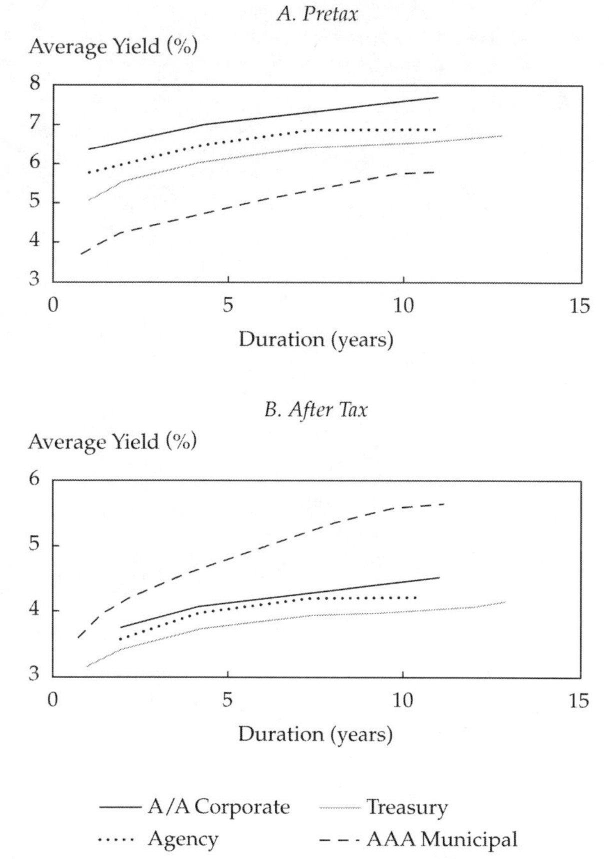

Notes: Corporate and municipal yields adjusted for credit transitions using Moody's Investors Service's transition rate. Based on income tax rates of 38.6 percent (federal) and 5 percent (state).

Sources: Based on estimates from Moody's Investors Service, Municipal Market Data Corporation, Salomon Smith Barney Yield Book, and Bernstein Investment Research and Management.

[1]For more on Moody's Investors Service's "transition rate," see http://riskcalc.moodysrms.com/US/research/trans/25097.pdf.

Figure 2. Average Yield of Various Bond Sectors for Investors in the AMT Bracket, January 1992–July 2002

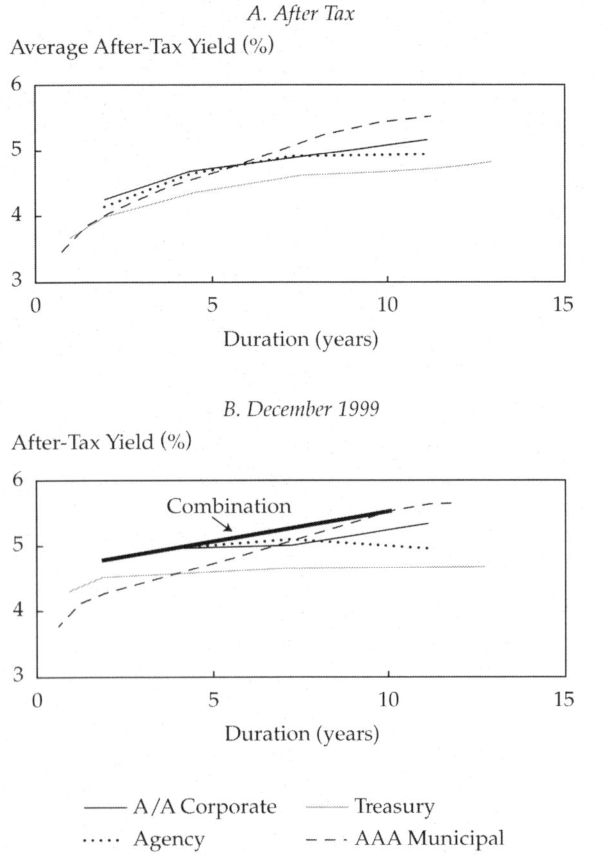

Notes: Corporate and municipal yields adjusted for credit transitions using Moody's Investors Service's transition rate. Based on AMT rate of 28 percent.

Sources: Based on estimates from Moody's Investors Service, Municipal Market Data Corporation, Salomon Smith Barney Yield Book, and Bernstein Investment Research and Management.

the intermediate municipal, corporate, agency, or Treasury market.

This combination of short-term taxable bonds and long-term municipals is usually the best solution for intermediate portfolios for which the client is subject to a 28 percent tax rate. A portfolio of 60 percent short agencies and 40 percent long municipals will typically offer from 12 to 25 bps more in income than any single sector solution—and without additional credit risk. Of course, such a strategy is not a "free lunch" because the manager is taking the price risk between the two different markets. Nonetheless, the manager can increase yield simply by paying attention to a client's tax bracket and picking the right bonds in the right maturity.

Capital Gains and Losses. Actively realizing gains and harvesting losses can also add after-tax value without appreciably changing the risk of the portfolio. For municipal bonds, the benefit of tax management is derived from realizing losses. Suppose a manager buys a $100 par value municipal bond with a 3 percent coupon and a six-year maturity, and six-year interest rates rise to 4 percent the next day. The bond's price will fall from par to $95.11, generating an unrealized loss of $4.89. If the manager holds the bond to maturity, no gain or loss will be incurred and the bond's after-tax compound return (over the six years to maturity, including the reinvested income at 4 percent) will be 3.10 percent, a little better than the original 3 percent yield because of the higher reinvestment rate.

But the manager also has the option to realize the $4.89 loss and reinvest the proceeds in a bond of similar maturity. Realizing the loss and sheltering a realized gain on another security is worth $1.98 (the tax savings at a 38.6 percent tax rate). The tax that would have been paid to the government can be reinvested in the portfolio, in which case the after-tax holding period return (over the six-year life of the bond) is 3.46 percent. So, harvesting losses does provide a free lunch. By realizing a loss, the investor is able to shelter a realized gain and thus reduce his or her tax liability, and by reinvesting the proceeds in tax-free bonds, can earn back the realized loss without paying income tax on the new security, or capital gains tax—if the new security is held to maturity.

Table 1 shows the value of harvesting losses for tax-exempt portfolios with 2-, 5-, 10-, and 20-year-average maturities at 1-, 5-, and 10-year investment horizons. To produce these numbers, a Monte Carlo simulation was used, with the percentage change in interest rates assumed to be normally distributed. For each maturity, the simulation began with interest rate levels that prevailed at the end of the second quarter of 2002 and randomly generated 3,000 possible outcomes, or "paths," based on the historical yield volatility of each maturity. Based on changes in yield, price changes were determined. At the end of the first year, half of the paths produced losses (rising interest rates) and half produced gains (falling interest rates). All losses were realized and the proceeds and the tax savings were reinvested at the higher interest rates. If a gain or no change in price occurred, the assumption was that the bond was held. For each of the 3,000 paths, a yield for the second year was generated using the yield at the end of year 1 and historical volatility. Based on yield changes in year 2, price changes were once again calculated and losses were realized if they existed. This exercise was followed for each year of the simulation.

Table 1. Value of Harvesting Losses for Municipal Bond Portfolios

	Top Tax Bracket			AMT Bracket		
Maturity (years)	1 Year	5 Years	10 Years	1 Year	5 Years	10 Years
2	0.30%	0.23%	0.23%	0.23%	0.19%	0.18%
5	0.58	0.44	0.42	0.46	0.36	0.34
10	0.93	0.68	0.65	0.72	0.55	0.52
20	1.20	0.89	0.82	1.00	0.73	0.68

Notes: Annualized percent return. Based on top income tax rate of 38.6 percent, AMT rate of 28 percent, long-term capital gains rate of 20 percent, and state income tax rate of 5 percent. Short-term losses were assumed to offset short-term gains, and long-term losses were assumed to offset long-term gains.

Source: Based on estimates from Bernstein Investment Research and Management.

This analysis reveals two patterns. First, the longer the average maturity of the portfolio, the more tax management is worth, because a long-term bond will incur a larger absolute loss than will a short-term bond. Second, the longer the investment horizon, the less tax management is worth, because the fraction of bonds with gains in the portfolio increases with the passage of time. In Year 1, half of the portfolios have a net loss and half have a net gain, but by Year 10, only 15–17 percent of the portfolios have a net loss. So, the value of harvesting losses diminishes over a long horizon but is still large, rivaling at each maturity the average management fee. To reiterate, the municipal bond market does indeed offer a free lunch!

Table 1 was calculated assuming that short-term losses were offsetting short-term gains. If losses were used to offset *long-term* gains, the values shown in Table 1 would be cut in half; the 42-bp benefit for the 5-year constant maturity portfolio at the 10-year horizon would drop to approximately 21 bps because long-term capital gains are taxed at essentially half the rate of short-term gains (20 percent versus the short-term capital gains tax rate of 38.6 percent). Still, 21 bps is about half of the average management fee in the private client market for intermediate-term bond portfolios, and it is there for the taking.

In lower tax brackets, the value of tax management lessens. But as shown in Table 1, harvesting losses in long-term municipal bonds for an investor subject to the AMT still offers significant value. As such, tax management should be part of the portfolio management process.

With taxable bonds, after-tax performance can be increased by realizing *both* gains and losses. The benefit is derived from the difference between the ordinary income and capital gains tax rates for individuals and the timing of tax payments. Say a manager invests $100 in a corporate bond with a 5 percent coupon and six-year maturity. As in the tax-exempt bond example, if interest rates rise by one percentage point the day after purchase, the price of the bond will fall by $4.63, generating an unrealized loss. If the manager chooses to hold the bond, the after-tax compound return (over the six-year life of the bond) will be 3.14 percent for an investor subject to the top tax bracket. If the bond is sold instead and the proceeds are reinvested in another taxable bond with a maturity of six years, the realized loss can offset a realized capital gain on another security, saving the investor $1.79 in taxes. The after-tax compound return for this second strategy is 3.25 percent, 11 bps higher than the first strategy. This savings is a consequence of the time value of money; the short-term gain that the loss sheltered is taxed at 38.6 percent and is payable today. The higher interest payments on the new bond are also taxed at 38.6 percent, but the taxes are not due until the interest payments are received in the future. The investor has effectively postponed the immediate payment of a 38.6 percent tax liability but will eventually pay the tax with future dollars over the life of the bond.

Harvesting losses in taxable bond portfolios does not always add value. Harvesting losses is advantageous (regardless of bond maturity) if the investor is offsetting realized short-term gains with realized short-term losses. Harvesting long-term losses to offset long-term gains, however, only adds value in longer bond maturities (19 years and longer). This is because a 20 percent capital gains tax is sheltered today in exchange for a higher tax (38.6 percent) on a higher interest payment (a 6 percent coupon versus a 5 percent coupon) in the future. Thus, this strategy works well for all maturities when short-term gains are offset by short-term losses, but when long-term gains are offset by long-term losses, the strategy works only for bonds with longer maturities.

What happens if the strategy is to take gains on taxable bonds? Assume a taxable bond was bought with a par value of $100, a 5 percent coupon, and a maturity of six years. Next, assume that interest rates plunged the day after purchase and six-year taxable yields fell from 5 percent to 4 percent, generating an unrealized gain of $4.89 on the bond. If the bond is held to maturity, it will yield an after-tax compound return of 2.99 percent to an investor subject to the top tax bracket. If, instead, the gain of $4.98 is realized after one year and a tax of $0.98 is paid (20 percent) and the proceeds are reinvested at 4 percent, the bond will earn a compound after-tax return of 3.10 percent if held to maturity. Once again, this is a pick-up of 11 bps. What happened? By selling the bond, the investor pays the long-term capital gains tax of 20 percent today but avoids a tax of 38.6 percent in the future on the 1 percent difference in the coupon income. (If this gain is sheltered by a loss, then the holding-period return jumps 3.26 percent, or 27 bps higher than buying and holding.)

How prudent is paying taxes today that do not really have to be paid until later? The benefit of lowering the tax bracket exceeds the time value of money for short- to intermediate-term bonds but not for long-term bonds, whose tax obligations arise only in the distant future. Beyond about a 15-year maturity, the value added from this type of strategy begins to decrease, totally dissipating at about a 30-year maturity. In general, it is not prudent to pay a tax today that can be paid later unless the tax rate today is a lot lower than it will be in the future.

Table 2 summarizes the value of tax management for taxable bonds when the investor is subject to both the highest tax rate and the AMT. If an individual is subject to the top federal income tax bracket and consistently has short-term gains, a high-turnover strategy of realizing short-term losses and long-term gains is highly profitable—the increased after-tax return is 50 bps for five-year bonds. The benefit of applying tax management for taxable bonds is lower for clients who are subject to the AMT.

Summary. By converting expected pretax returns (both income and capital gains components) to expected after-tax returns, managers can determine the best course of action for each client based on his or her tax situation. Considering the income component, municipal bonds are usually the best investment choice for investors in the top tax bracket. When the AMT rate applies, a manager can pick up an eighth to a quarter percent in after-tax yield by investing in a combination of tax-exempt and taxable bonds. Considering the capital gains component, harvesting losses on intermediate municipal bonds adds about 20–40 bps, whereas harvesting gains and realizing losses on intermediate taxable portfolios adds about 12–25 bps in value.

Broaden the Investment Universe

"The broader the investment universe, the better the investment results over time" is a general tenet of investing. Nevertheless, for the taxable investor, the best performing investment universe is simply municipal bonds. Often the universe is narrowed even further to the client's state of residence, even though nationally diversified municipal portfolios typically perform better than single-state portfolios. And as I have explained, the flexibility to invest in both taxable and tax-exempt portfolios can increase after-tax returns for clients subject to the top tax rate.

Home-State versus National Portfolio. About 50 percent of the municipal bond funds listed in Morningstar are single-state portfolios (excluding those in California and New York). Many investors invest only in their home state because they want to avoid paying state income tax, but they do so at the expense of reducing return. For a resident of Massachusetts, **Table 3** shows that the tax advantage of investing only in Massachusetts bonds is not substantial. An investor gives up about 0.07 percent in yield to buy a Massachusetts bond rather than a generic,

Table 2. Value of Harvesting Losses for Corporate Bond Portfolios

	Top Tax Bracket			AMT Bracket		
Maturity (years)	Increase	Due to Loss	Due to Gain	Increase	Due to Loss	Due to Gain
2	0.19%	0.02%	0.17%	0.08%	0.02%	0.06%
5	0.50	0.13	0.37	0.24	0.12	0.12
10	0.96	0.41	0.54	0.46	0.39	0.08

Notes: "Increase" is increase in after-tax return. Twenty percent yield volatility used for all maturities. Average option-adjusted yield from January 1992 to July 2002: 2-year yield, 6.37 percent; 5-year yield, 6.89 percent; and 10-year yield, 7.32 percent.

Sources: Based on estimates from Salomon Smith Barney Yield Book and Bernstein Investment Research and Management.

Table 3. Tax Advantage for Massachusetts Residents Who Invest in Only Massachusetts Bonds

	Massachusetts Insured	Generic Insured	Massachusetts Advantage
Yield (10-year)	4.09%	4.16%	(0.07)%
Less state tax (5.3%)	0.00	0.22	
Apparent after-tax yield	4.09	3.94	0.15
Plus federal tax offset (38.6%)	0.00	0.08	
Actual after-tax yield	4.09	4.02	0.07

Note: As of 1 July 2002.

Sources: Based on estimates from Municipal Market Data Corporation and Bernstein Investment Research and Management.

non-Massachusetts insured bond and saves about 22 bps in taxes. The after-tax yield pickup appears to be 15 bps, but that is not the end of the story. Most investors can deduct their state tax liability in computing their federal tax liability, which adds another 8 bps in after-tax yield to the generic tax-exempt bond. Therefore, the after-tax advantage of a Massachusetts resident investing in a Massachusetts bond is only 7 bps.

Table 4 shows the after-tax income benefit of a single-state municipal portfolio in a number of different states. On average, the extra after-tax yield from investing only in bonds from the state in which a client resides is 4 bps, or $400 per $1 million invested. Adhering to a single-state portfolio excludes, on average, 96 percent of the tax-exempt market—a narrow investment universe to say the least.

So, it should come as no surprise that, on average, nationally diversified portfolios provide about 20 bps in return over home-state portfolios (even after tax) and incur less risk because of the benefits of diversification. Furthermore, in the period from January 1992 to July 2002, the economy experienced incredible growth and minimal credit risk, thus probably understating the risk of home-state portfolios. Therefore, managers who take into account only the apparent income tax advantage of home-state portfolios are short-changing their clients. These managers should expand their investment universe to the national market to pick up additional return.

New York and California, however, are exceptions to the rule. New York and California each represent about 13 percent of the municipal bond market, which is much more than the 2 percent most states represent. Active management of portfolios dedicated to either of these states is viable because California and New York have diversified economies and a diverse group of issuers. In addition, their high state income tax rates make it even more advantageous for residents of those states to invest solely in their home state's bonds. Nonetheless, at Bernstein Investment Research and Management, we counsel residents of New York and California to invest outside of their home state once their in-state holdings reach 50 percent of their net worth. For example, a California-only portfolio has an after-tax return advantage of about 10 bps for a California resident but has more risk because of the lack of diversification outside of the state.

Table 4. After-Tax Advantage of a Single-State Municipal Bond Portfolio for Various States

State	Residents' Extra After-Tax Yield[a]	Percentage of National Muni Market
Connecticut	0.02%	1.6%
Florida	(0.01)	5.5
Illinois	0.00	4.6
Maryland	0.06	1.7
Massachusetts	0.07	3.7
New Jersey	0.09	3.5
Ohio	0.12	2.7
Pennsylvania	0.00	5.1
Texas	0.00	6.6
Virginia	0.05	2.2
Average	0.04%	3.7%

Notes: As of 1 July 2002. All bonds are insured AAA rated 10-year maturities.

[a]After federal tax offset, assuming top tax bracket.

Sources: Based on estimates from Merrill Lynch, Salomon Smith Barney, and Bernstein Investment Research and Management.

Beyond a Municipal-Only Portfolio. For investors in the top income tax bracket, taxable bonds do not provide a yield advantage over tax-exempt bonds. But as I mentioned earlier, the taxable and tax-exempt bond markets do not always move in sync, and periods arise when the tax-exempt yield advantage temporarily disappears at various points along the yield curve. As such, there should be some opportunities to add value by including taxable bonds in the investment universe. To gauge the scale of the opportunity, the performance of a seven-year-duration municipal index was calculated from 1992 through July 2002, resulting in before- and after-capital-gains-tax returns of 6.29 percent and 5.76 percent, respectively. (Taxes were considered because the index consists of bonds maturing in more than six years but less than eight years.) The after-tax performance of a seven-year-duration portfolio, optimally invested with perfect foresight in both tax-exempt and taxable (all investment-grade sectors) bond markets was calculated over the same time period and was found to be 8.93 percent. The portfolio was not burdened with transaction costs, and all gains and losses were assumed to be short term. Given the 3 percent after-tax advantage of the mixed tax-exempt/taxable portfolio, however, opportunity to outperform seems to be rampant. Even more surprising was that the perfect-foresight no-transaction-cost portfolio consisted of 60 percent municipals, 19 percent Treasuries, 11 percent corporates, and 10 percent agencies. This composition is surprising because at this duration, municipals typically offer 70 bps more in after-tax income than taxable bonds. This finding is incredible but also suspicious because the turnover of the portfolio was 900 percent.

Unfortunately, adding transaction costs of 2/32 for Treasuries, 1/8 for agencies, 1/4 for munis, and 3/8 for corporates cut the after-tax return premium of the perfect-foresight portfolio in half. After taxes and transaction costs, the portfolio's return dropped to 7.61 percent versus 6.29 percent for the municipal "buy and hold" portfolio and 5.76 percent for the municipal portfolio in which capital gains were consistently taken. The perfect-foresight with-transaction-cost portfolio in this scenario, on average, consisted of 57 percent municipals, 33 percent Treasuries, 9 percent agencies, and 1 percent corporates. The reduced use of corporates and agencies is not surprising given the transaction costs, but the fact that the municipal weighting did not rise (in fact, it fell) is surprising and suggests that cross-sector opportunities do exist for investors with the models and economies of scale to take advantage of relative yield swings.

Even with this evidence, buying taxable bonds for top-tax-bracket investors is difficult in practice because it usually means giving up the higher after-tax income of a municipal for an uncertain price advantage. With the advent of derivatives, this difficulty is becoming less of an issue, and more managers, particularly hedge fund managers, are adding value in taxable portfolios by taking advantage of the relationship between municipal and taxable bonds.

Even greater opportunity to add after-tax return exists for investors subject to lower tax brackets simply because the after-tax advantage of municipals is smaller. And at the AMT rate, the premium for the perfect-foresight with-transaction-cost portfolio jumped to more than 3 percent over the buy-and-hold municipal alternative.

By broadening the investment universe, managers can increase the after-tax returns of fixed-income portfolios. A simple change for many municipal bond investors subject to the top tax bracket would be investing in a nationally diversified portfolio rather than a single-state market. The sole exceptions to this rule are for taxpayers in California and New York. Nevertheless, they should remain cognizant of the risk associated with 100 percent exposure to their home state. Adding taxable bonds to the investment universe potentially offers additional sources of return, but because of transaction costs, the amount of excess return appears to be limited. Increasingly, derivative instruments are being used to capture this additional return and more efficiently take advantage of the changing relationship between municipal and taxable bonds.

For income reasons alone, an investor subject to the AMT should almost always hold short-term taxable bonds. But the benefit from switching between tax-exempt bonds and taxable bonds is especially strong for taxpayers subject to the AMT because of the lower AMT rate.

Performance Evaluation

If the goal is to add after-tax performance, managers should be prepared to report performance on an after-tax basis. Easily said, but from a back-office point of view, this is not easily done. AIMR has a committee studying this issue, and its recommendations are due soon. Currently, we work with our clients to establish the reporting rules. The most important rules are (1) choosing a benchmark that reflects the composition of a "normal" portfolio at the client's tax bracket and (2) determining if the after-tax performance will be reported on a realized or liquidation basis. On a realized basis, gains and losses are taxed only when realized; on a liquidation basis, both realized and unrealized capital gains and losses are taxed at the end of the reporting period.

Without standards, manager evaluation is a challenge. Most municipal bond managers historically have avoided taking capital gains. According to Morningstar, the average tax efficiency of municipal bond portfolio managers during the past 5 and 10 years is about 99 percent. As such, municipal bond portfolios for investors in the top tax bracket can be evaluated on a pretax basis. That said, the municipal market offers analysts its own peculiar issues.

The primary challenges to evaluating municipal bond portfolios are the lack of an accepted benchmark and the almost uniform distribution of portfolios across the maturity–risk spectrum. A number of performance measurement methods successfully used in other markets have been adopted in the municipal market, but when applied in the municipal market, these methods have several shortcomings.

Figure 3 depicts the return versus risk during the past 10 (Panel A) and 5 (Panel B) years for nationally diversified, high-grade municipal portfolios. Rating services often divide the market into short-, intermediate-, and long-term portfolio "buckets" or "peer groups." In the equity market, peer groups may have similar risks, but in the bond market, every incremental step in risk (maturity) typically yields additional return. Lipper Analytical Services and Morningstar address this relationship by creating peer groups based on risk and maturity. For example, Morningstar has three categories within the municipal market (short, intermediate, and long) and Lipper has four. Unfortunately, the categories are too broad. For example, the intermediate category of both Morningstar and Lipper essentially covers portfolios with average maturities of more than 5 years and less than 10 years. The interest rate risk of a 10-year bond is approximately 50 percent greater than that of a 5-year bond. Creating peer groups is not the solution. Imagine the extreme: In an effort to adjust more accurately for risk comparability, each portfolio would be analyzed versus other portfolios with the same historical risk—an impractical solution at best.

In an effort to adjust for interest rate risk, Sharpe ratios are also used to assess portfolio management skills. **Figure 4** demonstrates a typical pattern of Sharpe ratios for municipal bond portfolios over the past 10 (Panel A) and 5 years (Panel B). As you can see, analyzing the risk-and-return relationship as a Sharpe ratio basically inverts the yield curve so that, in general, the longer the portfolio's maturity (risk), the more it is penalized in terms of return—essentially the opposite of the problem experienced with peer group comparisons. In the bond market, Sharpe ratios are not the solution either.

Panel A of **Figure 5** shows the 10-year pre-management-fee returns for the same (high-grade, national) municipal bond portfolios shown in Figure 3. A market return line composed of 1-, 3-, 5-, 7-, 10-, and 20-year Lehman Brothers municipal indexes has also been added to the chart. With this addition, it is possible to measure the return difference between the portfolio and the market (i.e., the excess return) while accounting for each portfolio's historical risk. Panel B of Figure 5 goes further by isolating the excess return, or alpha, earned by active municipal portfolio managers over the past decade. This type of performance analysis makes the adjustment for interest rate risk that the other methods fail to do. To adjust for credit risk, the other primary risk in the municipal market, analysts should compare portfolios with return lines comprised of comparable bonds. For example, high-yield portfolios should be compared with high-yield return lines.

Figure 3. Risk and Return for Nationally Diversified High-Grade Municipal Bond Portfolios, as of 31 December 2001

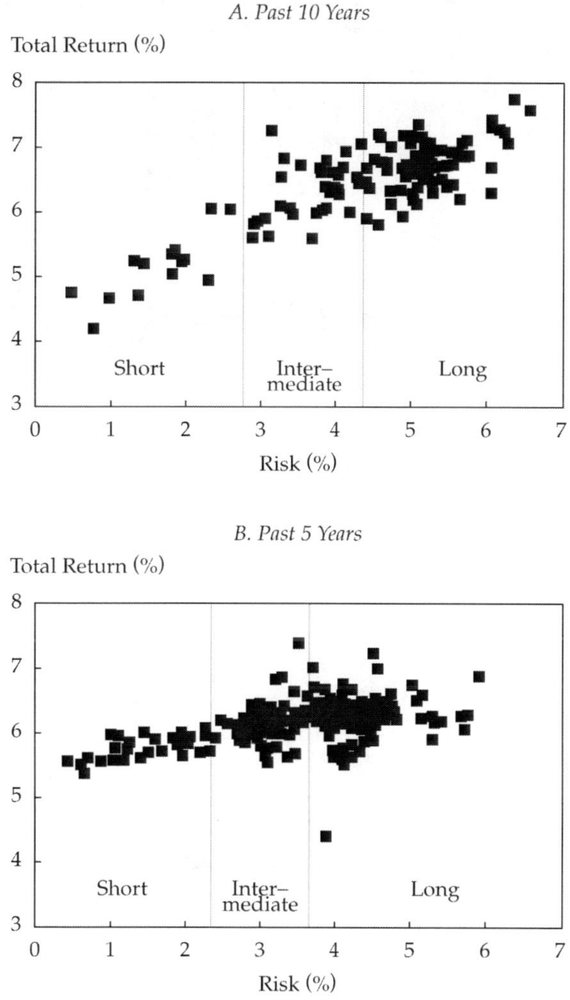

Note: Returns are before fees.

Sources: Based on estimates from Lehman Brothers, Morningstar, and Bernstein Investment Research and Management.

Figure 4. Sharpe Ratios for Nationally Diversified High-Grade Municipal Bond Portfolios, as of 31 December 2001

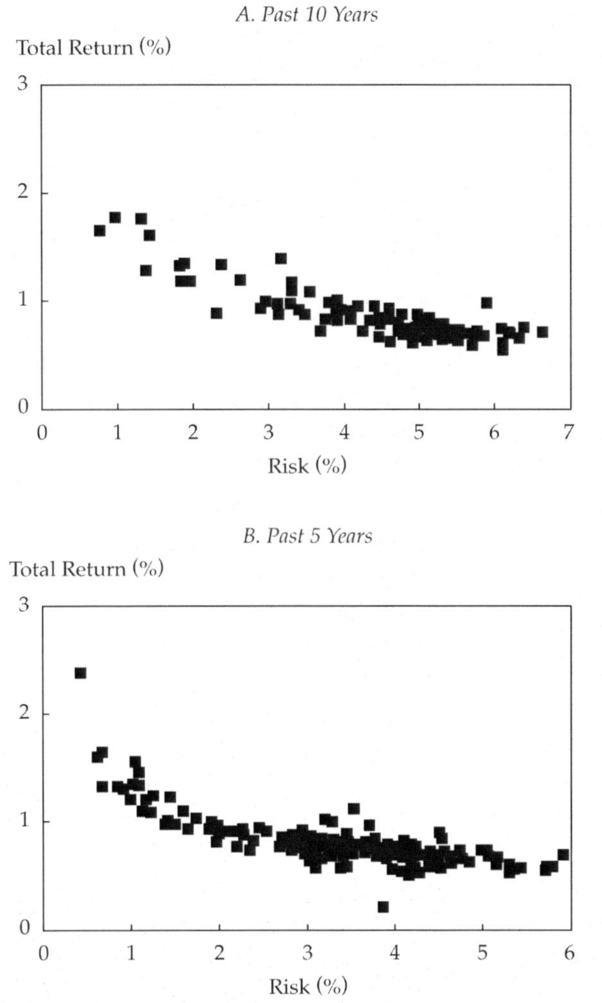

Note: Returns are before fees.

Source: Based on data from Morningstar.

Figure 5. Excess Return for Nationally Diversified High-Grade Municipal Bond Portfolios (for 10-year period ending 31 December 2001)

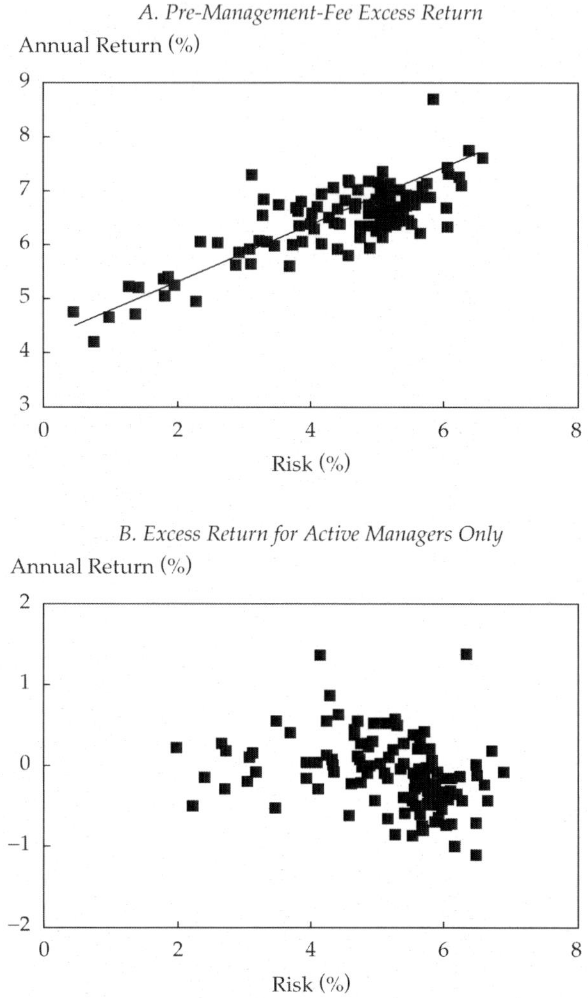

Sources: Based on estimates from Lehman Brothers, Morningstar, and Bernstein Investment Research and Management.

Conclusion

When managing bond portfolios for after-tax performance, investors should (1) exploit the gifts of the market and the tax code and (2) broaden the investment universe. Our results indicate that active tax management can add significant value to fixed-income portfolios over time. With municipal investments, portfolio managers can add value by "harvesting" losses. The value of this free lunch increases with maturity but decreases with the investment horizon.

Tax-managing taxable bonds takes advantage of the difference between the income and capital gains tax rates for individuals and the timing of tax payments. Unlike municipals, tax-managing taxable bonds entails realizing both gains and losses and is not sensitive to the investment horizon.

The added value of broadening the investment choices of taxable investors is also clear. At the very least, investors subject to the top tax bracket should not confine themselves to investing in the municipal bonds of their home state but should look at municipal issuers in all states to add value and reduce risk. While home-state investing has historically produced the highest value for residents of California and New York, those residents also should search nationally for value when home-state bond issues constitute the majority of their net worth. The benefits of including taxable bonds in the taxable investor's investment universe are less clear if transaction costs cannot be kept to a minimum.

The investment choices for investors subject to the AMT should include both municipal and taxable bonds. Owning short-term taxable bonds rather than municipals typically increases the after-tax income of a portfolio. Furthermore, greater opportunity to add value through cross-market trading exists simply because the after-tax advantage of municipals is smaller for AMT investors.

Performance should be reported and measured on an after-tax basis. And because tax management can *add* value to bond portfolios, tax management should be the approach that portfolio managers of taxable clients follow. Unfortunately, after-tax analysis of a manager's performance is challenging, at best, because the databases necessary to do it do not exist. This problem, however, is not a large obstacle for clients subject to the top tax bracket because municipal managers have historically been tax efficient.

The lack of an accepted benchmark and the almost uniform distribution of portfolios across the maturity–risk spectrum pose problems for performance evaluation in the municipal market. To adjust for duration differences and capture excess performance, analysts should compare municipal portfolios of similar credit quality with a municipal market return line that spans the maturity spectrum.

Made in United States
North Haven, CT
04 November 2026

21749008R00054